The Catholic Biblical Quarterly
Monograph Series
24

Creation in the Biblical Traditions

EDITED BY

Richard J. Clifford
and
John J. Collins

The Catholic Biblical Quarterly
Monograph Series
24

© The Catholic Biblical Association of America
Washington, DC 20064

Produced in the United States

Library of Congress Cataloging-in-Publication Data

Creation in the biblical traditions / edited by Richard J. Clifford
and John J. Collins
p.   cm.—(Catholic Biblical quarterly. Monograph Series : 24)
Includes bibliographical references and indexes.
Contents: Introduction, the theology of creation traditions /
Richard J. Clifford and John J. Collins — Creation theology in Genesis /
Bernard F. Batto — The demarcation of divine and human realms
in Genesis 2–11 / Robert A. Di Vito — Creation in the Psalms /
Richard J. Clifford — When form and content clash /
James L. Crenshaw — The theology of creation in Proverbs 8:22-31 /
Gale A. Yee — Creation and salvation in the Book of Wisdom /
Michael Kolarcik — Interpretations of the creation of the world
in Philo of Alexandria / Thomas L. Tobin — Creation in 4 Ezra /
Joan E. Cook.
ISBN 0-915170-23-X
1. Creation—Biblical teaching.   2. Cosmology, Biblical.
I. Clifford, Richard J.   II. Collins, John Joseph, 1946–
III. Series.
BS680.C69C73   1992
231.7′65′09014—dc
92-20268
CIP

Contents

RICHARD J. CLIFFORD, S.J.
JOHN J. COLLINS

Introduction: The Theology of Creation Traditions

The great flowering of biblical theology of the OT that took place in the 1960's had as its center Gerhard von Rad's two-volume *Old Testament Theology.*[1] For von Rad, history rather than nature revealed God. His volumes analyze the great historical works of the Bible, the Pentateuch, the Deuteronomistic History, the Chronicler, and the prophets who (in his view) reinterpreted those great streams of traditions. An earlier and influential essay of Von Rad had been even more radical: creation was a late import into the Bible that became significant only when linked to redemption, which always took place within history. Von Rad's early minimalist view of creation has not survived, partly due to his own implicit *retractio* in *Wisdom in Israel* in 1972.[2]

Today biblical theologians are respectful of the theological value of creation in its own right, finding the "natural" processes of the wisdom literature no less fertile *loci theologici* than the "history" of the historical books. It is not difficult to see why contemporary scholars make no apology for their interest in creation and no longer feel the need to subordinate it to redemption. Cosmogonies themselves are rich in meaning because in the ancient Near Eastern intellectual universe the origin of a phenomenon was a defining moment. That universe was not influenced by the modern idea of evolution that supposes that things begin in a simple state and gradually become more complex, more "perfect," in response

1. (New York: Harper, 1962, 1965), German original 1957, 1960.
2. (Nashville: Abingdon, 1972) *passim*.

1

to new situations. On the contrary, the essence or purpose of a particular entity, indeed of the universe, was given in the beginning. At that moment the imprint of the gods was clearest. There and then was fixed the way things worked. To know the origin was thus in a sense to know the divine intent. No wonder that creation in the Bible is such a rich vein for biblical theologians!

Cosmogonies occur in a variety of genres—hymns, incantations, astrological treatises, political tracts, epics. They explain why a temple is sacred to a god, why the heavens can be trusted to reveal feast days, why a certain god is king of the pantheon. The purpose of each text must be learned from the rhetorical aim of the genre in which it occurs. One must thus understand the genre and its historical development. The following paragraphs give a sketch of cosmogonies in the neighboring cultures of Israel—Egypt, Mesopotamia, and Canaan—as a prolegomenon to biblical accounts.

Egypt

Egyptian cosmogonies are attested as early as the mid-third millennium.[3] Though they did not directly influence the Bible,[4] they are worth a brief glance as an instance of ancient cosmogonic speculation; they are concrete, make ingenious use of analogy, and incorporate empirical observation. Egyptian mythology is not easy to understand, for it does not maintain a subject–object distinction and prefers image to concept. Cosmogonies were part of the theological systems of the major shrines, Heliopolis, Memphis, and Hermopolis, which sought to exalt their deity

3. Basic studies of Egyptian cosmogonies: S. Sauneron and J. Yoyotte, "La naissance du monde selon l'Egypte ancienne," in *La naissance du monde* (Sources Orientales 1; Paris: Seuil, 1959); P. Derchaine, "Kosmogonie" and J. Assmann, "Schöpfung," in *Lexikon der Ägyptologie* (ed. W. Helck and E. Otto; Wiesbaden: Harrassowitz, 1972–86) 3. 747–55 and 5. 677–90; E. Hornung, *Conceptions of God in Ancient Egypt* (tr. J. Baines; London: Routledge & Kegan Paul, 1983); B. Menu, "Les cosmogonies de l'ancienne Egypte," in *La création dans d'Orient Ancien* (LD 27; Congrès de l'ACFEB; Paris: Cerf, 1987) 97–116; J. P. Allen, *Genesis in Egypt: The Philosophy of Ancient Egyptian Creation Accounts* (Yale Egyptological Studies 2; New Haven: Yale, 1988).

4. J. Ebach makes a case for indirect influence on Genesis 1 *via* the cosmogony of Philo of Byblos, in *Weltentstehung und Kulturentwicklung bei Philo von Byblos: Ein Beitrag zur Überlieferung der biblischen Urgeschichte im Rahmen des altorientalischen und antiken Schöpfungsglaubens* (BWANT 108; Stuttgart: Kohlhammer, 1979) 35–37.

to the status of state god. Other cities borrowed from their traditions to make their own systems. Despite local diversity, scholars today agree the systems were not in rivalry and had an underlying unity.

Particularly Egyptian was the concept of nothingness, which was personified as Nun. Nun was inert, dark, watery; it was reckoned a monad, though Egyptian imagery wavered between self-development of the monad and a creator external to it. Before creation all was one. Creation was differentiation; the one became many. The creator god was "the one who makes millions." Nun remained after creation in two ways: outside the boundaries of the earth (imagined as a dry box of light surrounded by Nun) or inside, e.g., in ground water. The primal monad was thus both inert and generative.

Each system exalted its god as creator. In Heliopolis, Atum (a manifestation of the monad) generated the cosmic pair Shu and Tefnut by masturbation or (in a variant tradition) by spitting.[5] Memphis elevated its god Ptah, best illustrated in the Memphite Theology incised on the Shabaka Stone. On the analogy of Atum's creation by hand and seed, Ptah creates by teeth and lips, i.e., by word. The activity of Amun ("the hidden one") of Hermopolis, which is described with remarkable subtlety in the Papyrus Leiden, comes very close to modern ideas of transcendence.

Explicit attention to the creation of the human race is late in Egypt. The old cosmogonies assume that the race emerges with the world.

Mesopotamia

Sumerian cosmogonies, according to the scholar who has done the most to systematize them, Jan van Dijk, belong to one of two traditions.[6] In the Nippur tradition creation takes place in the cosmic marriage between Heaven (An) and Earth (Ki): An brings Ki to flower by raining upon her. As earth blooms, the human race emerge from the soil loosened by the hoe, *emersio* in van Dijk's terminology. The marriage act took place at

5. Another example of experiential thinking is the primeval mound (Ta-Tenen, "The land that rises"), which is imaginatively derived from the little mounds teeming with life that is left by the Nile receding from its annual flood.

6. The Nippur traditions are discussed in "Le motif cosmique dans la pensée sumérienne," *AcOr* 28/1–2 (1964) 1–59, and the Eridu traditions in "Sumerische Religion," *Handbuch der Religionsgeschichte* (ed. J. P. Asmussen *et al.*; Göttingen: Vandenhoeck & Ruprecht, 1971), 1. 450, 466–70.

Dur-an-ki ("bonding of heaven and earth"), a site in the temple of Nippur. Nippur was the city of Enlil, the god of earth, who first separated the cosmic pair. The Nippur system included a pre-creation phase — an embryonic period of father and mother gods. In the other system, that of Eridu, the water god Enki creates by bringing up the underground waters *via* rivers and canals to fertilize the earth. The act was imagined in sexual terms: the fertilizing water was the semen of Enki the bull. The act included implicitly human beings, for cities came into being along the river banks. A separate creation of man is narrated in the poem Enki and Ninmah: Enki, with the help of the mother goddess, creates human beings from clay, *formatio* according to van Dijk.

Cosmogonies in the Akkadian language range in date from the second to the mid-first millennia. Most of the fifteen or so examples are brief and narrowly functional, i.e., tied to a single operation, e.g., to cure an ailment, to dedicate a temple, to provide background for a literary debate between newly created beings, to show heavenly bodies are divine signs for the human race.[7] A good example is the well-known incantation against a toothache in which the magician narrates the creation of the world, telling how the worm was assigned to eat fruit. The worm has deviated from that task to gnaw at human gums and so the magician prays the god to make the worm leave the sufferer's mouth and return to its original purpose of eating fruit.[8]

Several creation accounts transcend strictly functional aims by being integrated into a long story with a broadly historical or exploratory aim, e.g., Atrahasis, Enuma elish, The Sumerian Flood Story,[9] and The Rulers

7. Several are conveniently collected in J. Bottero, "Antiquités Assyro-Babyloniennes," *Annuaire École Pratique des Hautes Études* Sec. IV, 1978–79 (Paris: Klincksieck, 1982) 85–135, reprinted in *Mythes et rites de Babylone* (Bibliothèque de l'École des hautes études, Sec. IV, Sciences historiques et philologiques 328; Paris: Slatkine-Champion, 1985) 279–328. Some have recently been reedited and translated in J. Bottéro and S. N. Kramer, *Lorsque les dieux faisaient l'homme: mythologie mésopotamienne* (Bibliothèque des histoires; Paris: Gallimard, 1989). See also M.-J. Seux, "La création du monde et de l'homme dans la littérature Suméro-Akkadienne," in *La Création* 41–78, and see n. 9.

8. *ANET,* 100–101.

9. M. Civil in W. G. Lambert and A. R. Millard, *Atra-ḫasīs: The Babylonian Story of the Flood* (Oxford: Clarendon, 1969) 138–45; S. N. Kramer, "The Sumerian Deluge Myth," *Anatolian Studies* 33 (1983) 115–121; G. Pettinato, *Das altorientalische Menschenbild und die sumerischen und akkadischen Schöpfungsmythen* (Heidelberg: Winter, 1971)

of Lagash.[10] Atrahasis (about 1245 lines in one Old Babylonian version of the seventeenth century B.C.) and Enuma elish (ca. 1100 lines of probably the twelfth century B.C.) use venerable traditions for literary and political aims. Atrahasis explores overpopulation, drawing on the traditions of Enki the creator and of the flood. Enuma elish exalts Marduk as head of the pantheon by showing that he is the legitimate successor to Ea and Enlil; it draws on Ninurta traditions. Whether Enuma elish has influenced the Bible directly is controverted but there is no doubt of the influence of Atrahasis. The fact deserves further comment.

Atrahasis blends two traditions. In the first, Enki creates the human race (from clay and the blood of a god) as substitute workers for the unwilling lower class of gods; in the second, the human race expands with such noise that the gods get no rest and angrily send plagues, culminating in a flood, to wipe them out. All except the last plague are thwarted by Enki; against the flood he can only rescue his client Atrahasis in a boat. The gods, quickly learning how much they need the race, change their minds and bid Enki create again but this time with inbuilt population control—childbirth demons, a class of celibate women, and mortality.[11] The similarity of the plot to Genesis 2–9 cannot be missed and in fact was noticed as soon as all the tablets were published in 1969.

34–35, 97–100; T. Jacobsen, "The Eridu Genesis," *JBL* 100 (1981) 513–29 and *The Harps that Once . . . : Sumerian Poetry in Translation* (New Haven: Yale: 1987) 143–150; P. D. Miller, "Eridu, Dunnu, and Babel: A Study in Comparative Mythology," *HAR* 9 (1985) 227–251. The hellenistic author Berossus transmits a brief version. See S. M. Burstein, *The Babyloniaca of Berossus* (Sources and Monographs: Sources from the Ancient Near East 1/5; Malibu: Undena, 1978).

10. E. Sollberger, "The Rulers of Lagaš," *JCS* 21 (1967) 279–86.

11. For the general interpretation, see W. L. Moran, "Some Considerations of Form and Interpretation in *Atra-Hasis*," in *Language, Literature, and History: Philological and Historical Studies Presented to Erica Reiner* (AOS Monograph 67; ed. F. Rochberg-Halton; Winona Lake: Eisenbrauns, 1987) 245–55. For mortality as a post-flood institution, see W. G. Lambert, "The Theology of Death," *Death in Mesopotamia* (Mesopotamia 8; ed. B. Alster; XXVIᵉ Rencontre assyriologique internationale; Copenhagen: Akademisk, 1980) 58. His suggestion has been accepted by T. Jacobsen, "Death in Mesopotamia," ibid., W. L. Moran, "Some Considerations," 254, C. Wilcke, "Göttliche und menschliche Weisheit im Alten Orient," *Weisheit: Archäologie der literarischen Kommunikation III* (Munich: Fink, 1991) 260, and J. Bottéro, in Bottéro, *Lorsque les dieux,* 528.

Canaan

In the Ugaritic texts, written before 1200 B.C., the high god El has the epithet "creator of creatures/creation" (*bny bnwt*) and "father of man" (*'b 'dm*), and his wife Asherah has the epithet "creator of the gods" (*bnyt 'lm*). The epithets occur generally in appeals to the god's mercy, something like "Help those you have borne!" The Ugaritic verb **banaya* has the same wide range as Akkadian *banû,* from "build (a building)" to "beget."

Six lengthy but partially preserved clay tablets describe cosmic battles between the storm god Baal and his enemies Sea or Death and the temple that is built to memorialize that victory. The victory of the storm God Yahweh over Sea in the Bible is cosmogonic (see Psalms 77, 89, 94, 96) but the victory of Baal cannot strictly be proven to be cosmogonic in the Ugaritic texts.[12] The problem is that Baal remains subject to El, who is the creator. Until the puzzling relationship between the old patriarch and the young warrior is cleared up, the question whether Baal is a creator is unanswerable. It is well known that Yahweh in the Bible is portrayed with the traits of both El and Baal.

A few inscriptions mention "El creator of the earth." The eighth-century Phoenician text from Karatepe in Cilicia threatens would-be defacers of the monument: iii.18"May Baal Shamem, and El Creator of the Earth (*'l qn 'rṣ*) 19 and Eternal Sun and all the assembly of the sons of the gods efface that kingdom and that king and iv.1that man who is a man of renown" (*KAI* 26). The only other epigraphic mention is a Neo-Punic dedicatory plaque of the early second century A.D., where the name and epithet occur alone (*KAI* 129). A similar phrase appears in Genesis 14:18, *'ēl 'elyôn qōneh šāmayim wā'āreṣ,* "El Elyon creator of heaven and earth." In the Karatepe curse, El is named after Baal Shamem (probably the storm-god Baal Hadad[13]) and before Eternal Sun and the assembly of the gods.[14] Baal is invoked at the beginning of his inscription and that priority

12. For a summary of the question, see R. J. Clifford, "Cosmogonies in the Ugaritic Texts," *Or* 53 (1984) 183–201, who was then less cautious regarding Baal as creator. For a different approach and recent bibliography, see J.-L. Cunchillos, "Peut-on parler de mythes de création à Ugarit?" in *La Création,* 79–96.

13. For Baal Shamem as Baal Hadad, cf. M. Barré, *The God-List in the Treaty between Hannibal and Philip V of Macedonia: A Study in Light of the Ancient Near Eastern Treaty Tradition* (Baltimore: Johns Hopkins, 1983) 40–57.

14. The assembly is sometimes addressed as a distinct entity in Phoenician inscriptions, as in *KAI* 4.4–5; 10.10, 16.

apparently carries over into the later curse. The inscription supports the conclusions from the Ugaritic texts, where only El is unambiguously called creator and Baal is patron of kings and lord of the fertility-bestowing storm.

The last piece of evidence is the cosmogony of Sakkunyaton, an otherwise unknown ancient worthy. It was transmitted by the late first-century A.D. writer Philo of Byblos and preserved in the *Praeparatio evangelica* of the fourth-century A.D. patristic author Eusebius of Caesarea.[15] According to the text, the universe began when a cosmic wind came into contact with moist and boundless stuff. Initial movement of the elements is explained on the analogy of sexual desire. The dynamism of creation is wholly immanent and modeled on human behavior. Philo's cosmogony appears to be eclectic, incorporating elements from Phoenician, Greek, and Egyptian traditions. It bears some resemblance to Genesis 1.

Several conclusions from our survey of cosmogonies of Israel's neighbors are relevant for the Bible. Perhaps the most obvious is the ancient poets' assumption that the originating moment explains the present. That moment grounds or explains something experienced here and now—the sacredness of a temple, the status of a god, the authority of a king. Cosmogonies are not told for their own sakes, out of a modern scientific interest, to explain "exactly how it happened." The genre is the best clue to their aim. One must be prepared for a wide variety of genres—hymns, incantations, astrological treatises, epics.

A corollary of the first conclusion is the general interest in the pre-creation period. The scenario of the Sumerian Nippur tradition has, according to van Dijk, a pre-creation embryonic period. In the Eridu tradition, the pre-creation tableau that opens The Dilmun Myth (Enki and Ninhursaga) is a mirror image of creation, e.g., "At Dilmun, no crow cries 'ka'gu,' no francolin [type of partridge] goes 'dardar,' no lion kills, no wolf takes a lamb. Unknown is the dog herding the goats, unknown is the pig, eater of grain. The widow does not spread malt on the roof, no bird in the sky forages for it," etc.[16] In Egypt, Nun, undifferentiated

15. On this difficult text, cf. A. I. Baumgarten, *The Phoenician History of Philo of Byblos: A Commentary* (Études préliminaires aux religions orientales dans l'Empire romain; Leiden: Brill, 1981); J. Ebach, *Weltentstehung* (see n. 5); H. W. Attridge and R. A. Oden, *Philo of Byblos The Phoenician History: Introduction, Critical Text, Translation, Notes* (CBQMS 9; Washington: Catholic Biblical Association, 1981).

16. Clifford's rendering of the translation of Pascal Attinger, "Enki et Ninhursaga," *ZA* 74 (1984) 7–9.

potential, persists even after the act of creation and is found both outside all boundaries and inside the world (in certain situations). Several Akkadian texts imagine the period before creation as characterized by unbounded water. One text begins, "A holy house, a house of the gods, had not been built in (its) holy place," and goes on to list other basic entities that had not been created such as trees and reeds, dry land, and the human race. Unlike the Egyptian poets who imagined the *Urstoff* abstractly, Mesopotamian poets imagined the period concretely and specifically as the *absence* of essential elements of their everyday universe.

A third conclusion from our survey is that cosmogonies are commonly functional, part of an operation like praying, casting a spell, dedicating a temple, interpreting the stars. The legitimating and explaining role of cosmogonies is transcended when the cosmogony becomes incorporated into a narrative. The Akkadian epics Atrahasis and Enuma elish make cosmogonies part of their treatment of overpopulation and of their exalting Marduk as king of the gods. The Leiden papyrus waxes almost philosophical as it portrays Amun as the creator of all who has taken over other gods' functions.

A fourth conclusion is that no good evidence exists for the view that there were two distinct traditions of creation, one of creation of the world and the other of creation of human beings. Such a distinction between *Weltschöpfung* and *Menschenschöpfung* has become a common assumption. Claus Westermann assumed it in his analysis of Second Isaiah and Psalms[17] and his students have applied the distinction in their work on Second Isaiah, Psalms and Wisdom Literature.[18] Such a distinction neglects the fact that in ancient Near Eastern literature the creation of human beings is part of a system of world creation. In Sumerian, the Nippur tradition has human beings emerge from the fertilized earth (*emersio*) and the Eridu tradition has Enki form human beings from moistened

17. *Isaiah 40–66: A Commentary* (Philadelphia: Westminster, 1969) 24–26 and *Genesis 1–11: A Commentary* (Minneapolis: Augsburg, 1984) 19–25. This separation is part of Westermann's form critical conclusions: creation of the world is found in the genre of hymn and forms the basis of praise; creation of human beings appears in the genre of individual lament including the *Heilsorakel*. Second Isaiah brought the two traditions together.

18. R. Albertz, *Weltschöpfung und Menschenschöpfung untersucht bei Deuterojesaja, Hiob und in den Psalmen* (Calwer Theologischen Monographien A/3; Stuttgart: Calwer, 1974) and P. Doll, *Menschenschöpfung und Weltschöpfung in der alttestamentlichen Weisheit* (Stuttgarter Bibelstudien 117; Stuttgart: Katholisches Bibelwerk, 1985).

earth (*formatio*). The creation of human beings can occasionally be the subject of a separate account, as in the Sumerian Enki and Ninmah or in the Akkadian Atrahasis, but occasional separate treatment does not imply separate and distinct traditions. Egyptian thought assumes human beings are created along with the universe[19] even though exclusive attention to the creation of human beings is rare and late. Westermann's further claim that the creation accounts of individual elements (as opposed to the world) are older has no support from ancient Near Eastern texts. Quite the opposite is true. Even the oldest Sumerian cosmogonies, which are detectible in third-millennium god lists, are systems that include the creation of the human race.[20]

The fifth and final consideration is important for biblical theologians: the differences between the ancient Near Eastern and modern definitions of creation. Failure to be clear about ancient and modern differences has obscured the role of ancient cosmogonies in the Bible. Ancient cosmogonies differ in at least four ways from modern concepts of creation: the process, the product or emergent, the description, and the criteria for truth.[21]

Process. Ancient Near Eastern writers usually imagined divine creation on the model of human making or natural activity. The gods mold the world like clay; they form mountains and bring forth streams from dragons' bodies; they build the world like a building; their word causes something to exist; cosmic elements like heaven or earth or rivers beget other elements; a hillock arises from a flood. Frequently cosmogony is imagined as a conflict of beings endowed with wills in which the creator god vanquishes inert or hostile forces.

Modern people, influenced by scientific and evolution thinking, regard creation as the impersonal interaction of physical forces extending over eons. They reject any psychologizing of the process. Ancient texts do not make the modern dichotomous distinction between "nature" and humans and sometimes offer psychic and social explanations for non-human phenomena.

Product or emergent. To the ancients, organized human society (or an aspect of it) emerged from the creation process. To moderns, on the

19. J. Assmann, "Schöpfung," *Lexikon der Ägyptologie* 5. 678.
20. J. van Dijk, "Le motif cosmique" (see n. 6).
21. These comments below are drawn from Clifford, "The Hebrew Scriptures and the Theology of Creation," *TS* 46 (1985) 507–523.

other hand, creation usually issues in the physical world, typically the planet amid the solar system. Community and culture do not generally come into consideration. If life is discussed in connection with creation, it is usually life in the most primitive biological sense.

Manner of reporting. Ancient texts often report creation as drama; moderns write scientific reports. The difference is a consequence of two different conceptualizations. Modern conceptualizing of the process is generally evolutionary and "impersonal," operating with the assumption of laws of nature. The ancients often interpreted the process on the analogy of human activity, quite frequently a conflict of wills; the result was drama or story. The manner of reporting corresponds in each case to the underlying conception of the process. Each approach advances the thought and resolves problems in different fashion. Scientists offer new hypotheses as new data have to be explained. Ancients devised new stories, or wove variations into existing ones when they wished to explain fresh elements of their world. It is not always easy for moderns, for whom a story normally is either entertainment or illustration, to regard the story itself as a carrier of serious meaning. A special difficulty for modern thinkers is the ancient tolerance of many stories for the same event. Sumerian literature had two different cosmogonic systems and Akkadian literature preserved at least thirteen different "minor cosmogonies" in addition to Enuma elish and Atrahasis. Egypt had as many systems as major sanctuaries. The Bible contains quite different cosmogonies in Genesis, Proverbs, Job, Psalms, and Second Isaiah.

Criterion of truth. Moderns expect a creation story to be able to explain all the data and be compatible with other verified theories and data. Failure to do so makes a hypothesis suspect. There is a drive toward complete and coherent explanation. The criterion of truth for ancient cosmogonies, on the other hand, is dramatic or functional—plausibility or suitability. In one sense the criterion is no less empirical than the scientific account since it draws upon direct observation of the world but its verisimilitude is measured differently. Drama selects, omits, concentrates; it need not render a complete account or cohere with other versions. The story can concentrate on a single event and leave others out of consideration. Enuma elish is interested in Marduk's rule over the gods and over Babylon, Atrahasis, in the balance of earthly resources and human population, and Psalm 89, in locating Davidic kingship in the very creation of the world.

The ancient Near Eastern traditions of creation take on a new setting and meaning in the biblical context. Yahweh, the God of Israel, is the sole deity; the focus of interest is earth and the doings of the human race, not heaven and the doings of the gods. Yahweh's holiness makes an ethical claim on Israel. The early biblical treatments of creation, however, share the narrative form and dramatic function of the ancient myths. The classic story of creation and primeval history in Genesis resembles Atrahasis both in style and in plot.[22] The appeal is to imagination rather than to philosophical reason. Allusions to creation in the poetic books of the Bible also presuppose a mythical narrative, usually of the Canaanite type.[23] The depiction of Yahweh as storm god in Psalms 77, 89, 93, 97 and 98 recalls the conflict of Baal and Sea in the Ugaritic myth. Second Isaiah clearly reflects a similar narrative of a battle with the dragon and the sea (Isa 51:9–10). The Israelite adaptation of Canaanite cosmogonic myth also forms the backdrop for the anguished reflections of Job (cf. Job 26:12; 41:1), although the acute sense of human limitation in that book underlines the elusive, metaphorical character of the theological discourse.[24] The narrative form dominates Israelite thinking about creation down through the exilic period.

We find the beginnings of a transition in the Book of Proverbs. Proverbs 8 has a narrative, in which personified Wisdom appears as a character, and its treatment of creation is highly metaphorical.[25] Yet the brief autobiographical narrative of Wisdom does not describe interactions with any other characters in concrete detail. Wisdom does not lose its character as an abstract noun, a property of God, or of the universe, or of humanity, rather than an independently existing goddess or heavenly being. This sense of a property of creation (however elusive) appears with less personification in Job 28. Von Rad appropriately described this figure of Wisdom as "the self-revelation of Creation."[26] In short, Wisdom is a metaphysical category, inferred by abstraction from the experience of wisdom in human affairs and the phenomenon of order in the universe. It is not yet the subject of philosophical speculation in Proverbs, but it

22. See the contributions of Bernard Batto and Robert Di Vito in this volume.
23. See the contribution of Richard Clifford.
24. See the essay of James Crenshaw, below.
25. See the contribution of Gale Yee.
26. Von Rad, *Wisdom in Israel*, 144–76.

provides a crucial category for the later rapprochement between the biblical tradition and Greek philosophy.

The beginnings of this rapprochement can be seen in the book of Sirach. Sirach, like Proverbs, puts an autobiographical narrative in the mouth of Wisdom, and makes liberal use of metaphors in Sirach 24. The narrative evokes the biblical history from creation to the establishment of Zion and is not notably philosophical. The opening statement attributed to Wisdom, however, is a pregnant one: "I came forth from the mouth of the Most High" (Sir 24:3). While this statement recalls the process of creation in Genesis 1, it also paves the way for the identification of Wisdom as either Word (λόγος) or spirit (πνεῦμα), terms which had rich connotations in Greek philosophy. Philosophical influence can be detected elsewhere in Sirach's reflections on creation. At Sir 33:14, he offers an extraordinary comment on the way the world is constituted: "Good is the opposite of evil, and life the opposite of death; so the sinner is the opposite of the godly. Look at all the works of the Most High; they come in pairs, one the opposite of the other." Evil, in short, has its necessary place in the divine order of things. This statement is hard to reconcile with Sirach's reading of the Genesis story, elsewhere in the book, which emphasizes the goodness of creation (16:26–30) and human responsibility for sin (15:11–20). It is remarkably similar, however, to the contention of the Stoic Chrysippus that "There is absolutely nothing more foolish than those who think that there could have been goods without the co-existence of evils. For since goods are opposite to evils, the two must necessarily exist in opposition to each other and supported by a kind of opposed interdependence. And there is no such opposite without its matching opposite."[27] Again, the long hymn in praise of the works of the Lord (42:15–43:33) emphasizes the conformity of nature to the will of its Maker, and culminates with the declaration: "He is the all" (43:27). Again there is striking similarity to Stoic thought, as evidenced by Cleanthes' *Hymn to Zeus*.[28] Ben Sira, of course, was no pantheist, nor did he subscribe to a consistent Stoic philosophy. He was seeking, however,

27. A. A. Long and D. N. Sedley, *The Hellenistic Philosophers. Vol. 1. Translations of the Principal Sources. with Philosophical Commentary* (Cambridge: Cambridge University, 1987) 329.

28. Ibid., 326–27. See the comments of Martin Hengel, *Judaism and Hellenism* (Philadelphia: Fortress, 1974) 1. 147–48; R. Pautrel, "Ben Sira et le Stoicisme," *RSR* 51 (1963) 535–49.

to give a coherent and rationally satisfying account of creation, and so he experimented with philosophical notions. To be sure, his philosophizing is rudimentary, and even self-contradictory on occasion,[29] but nonetheless he marks a milestone in Jewish reflection on the problem of creation.

The attempt to reformulate biblical tradition in Hellenistic categories is taken much farther in the Wisdom of Solomon. The perspective of Wisdom extends to the story of the Exodus and even to the final judgment.[30] History, however, is viewed from the perspective of creation. Throughout, Wisdom attempts to give a coherent account of the workings of the cosmos. Pivotal to that coherence is the notion of Wisdom, which is described in terms reminiscent of the Stoic Logos as "that which holds all things together" ("the spirit of the Lord," 1:7) and which "reaches mightily from one end of the earth to the other and orders all things well" (8:1).[31] Creation is thus programmed by Wisdom to defend the righteous and punish the wicked. Even the apparently miraculous events of the Exodus do not require a disruption of the laws of nature.

Again, Wisdom is no Stoic treatise. It insists on the transcendence of the creator, in accordance with traditional Judaism. Like Philo, Wisdom finds its philosophical milieu in Middle Platonism rather than in Stoicism, as it also incorporates elements of the Platonic tradition which were more congenial to a theology of transcendence. Creation is understood to point beyond itself: "from the greatness and beauty of created things comes a corresponding perception of their Creator" (13:5). While Wisdom insists on the role of the creator, however, it does not envisage *creatio ex nihilo.* Rather, the world is created "from formless matter" (11:17), which was apparently eternal.[32] This formulation, of course, was compatible with Genesis 1, where the formless earth can be understood as the raw material of creation. The doctrine of *creatio ex nihilo* does not emerge until second-century Christianity.[33]

---

29. Compare the diverse approaches that Sirach entertains on the subject of theodicy. See J. Crenshaw, "The Problem of Theodicy in Sirach: On Human Bondage," *JBL* 94 (1975) 47–64. A more positive, enthusiastic appreciation of Sirach's achievement can be found in Burton Mack, *Wisdom and the Hebrew Epic* (Chicago: University of Chicago, 1985).

30. See the essay of Michael Kolarcik in this volume.

31. David Winston, *The Wisdom of Solomon* (AB 43; Garden City: Doubleday, 1979) 104, 189–90.

32. See ibid., 38–39.

33. Ibid., 40.

The Wisdom of Solomon insists on the goodness of God's creation: "he created all things that they might exist and the generative forces of the world are wholesome" (1:14). It deviates from biblical tradition, however, and contrasts sharply with Sirach, in the assertion that "God did not make death" (1:13). The exclusion of death from creation undoubtedly simplifies the goodness of creation, required by Genesis. It opens the way, however, for an element of dualism, which is more characteristic of apocalypticism than of wisdom in the Jewish tradition.

The philosophical reinterpretation of biblical tradition on creation becomes full-fledged in the works of Philo of Alexandria. There are still traces of a mythological conception in Philo's understanding of the Logos, which can on occasion be called "Chief of the Angels,"[34] but his work is grounded in Greek philosophy to a far greater extent than is the case with the Wisdom of Solomon. In the *De Opificio Mundi*, creation is treated systematically as a philosophical problem, for the first time in Jewish tradition. Ultimately, the philosophical idiom of Philo, rather than the narrative idiom of Genesis, would dominate the discussion of creation in Christian theology, down to recent times.

The development from mythic narratives to systematic philosophy is the most important aspect of the discussion of creation at the end of the Old Testament period. This development was not uniform, however. The philosophically oriented wisdom literature was only one of several genres to flourish in the Hellenistic period. Another major strand of Jewish literature is found in the apocalyptic literature, which is represented in this volume by Joan Cook's essay on Fourth Ezra. The apocalypses retain much more of the narrative form of the older creation traditions. Fourth Ezra is somewhat atypical, however, in its focus on the Genesis story of Adam. The Enoch tradition, in contrast, focuses on the story of the fallen angels as the paradigmatic event of primeval history. The Enoch literature, however, is greatly concerned with the order of nature, and one whole treatise is devoted to the movements of the stars (1 Enoch 72–82).[35] This literature is pervaded with the sense that human destiny is bound up with the order of the cosmos. Like the Wisdom of Solomon, the Enoch literature views the cosmos as a whole, but unlike the wisdom book, the apocalypses

34. See the essay of Thomas H. Tobin, below.
35. On the cosmological interests of the Enoch tradition see James C. VanderKam, *Enoch and the Growth of an Apocalyptic Tradition* (CBQMS 16; Washington: Catholic Biblical Association, 1984) 76–109.

typically see the creation as spoiled by sin, and in need of judgment and redemption.[36]

Fourth Ezra stands in a somewhat ambivalent relation to the older apocalyptic tradition, and is, indeed, also deeply indebted to wisdom traditions. Like Sirach, it looks to the story of Adam as the paradigm of human conduct, but is more pessimistic than Sirach about humanity's evil inclination. Unlike Sirach, however, it hesitates to affirm the goodness of creation. Ezra brings no philosophical categories to bear on the problem of evil. Instead, he finally accepts the apocalyptic solution to the problem, which offers a vision of the future rather than a justification of the present. According to 4 Ezra, the Most High made not one world but two (7:50). At the appropriate time, this world will be returned to primeval silence for seven days, and the hidden world will be revealed. The visions of this new world in chaps 11–13 finally cause Ezra to lose sight of the apparent injustice of the first creation.

It is apparent from the essays in this volume that there is no single theology of creation in the Old Testament. It is also apparent that there is a persistent concern throughout this corpus with understanding the way the world and humanity came into being. The ultimate beginning, like the Creator, lies beyond the horizon of empirical human knowledge. All any generation can do is construct a picture in accordance with the best resources of its time. For much of ancient Israel, these resources were provided by the great mythic narratives of the ancient Near East, which were adapted to meet the demands of biblical monotheism. At a later time, Greek philosophy appeared to provide categories that were more intellectually satisfying. These categories later provided the underpinning for traditional Christian systematic theology. Even though the philosophical categories appear more rational, however, they too are human constructs, with no exclusive access to truth. If Marduk and Tiamat are alien to modern scientific cosmology, so is the Logos of the Stoics. The Big Bang theory of modern physics may yet seem antiquated to future generations. It is salutary to bear in mind that even in the Hellenistic age, some Jewish sages still had need of the imaginative cosmology of the apocalypses. In the end, no theory of creation is definitive. Yet Solomon's attempt to comprehend "the beginning and end and middle of times" (Wis 7:18) remains an indispensible part of the faith that seeks understanding.

36. See John J. Collins, "Cosmos and Salvation. Jewish Wisdom and Apocalyptic in the Hellenistic Age," *HR* 17 (1977) 121–42.

BERNARD F. BATTO

Creation Theology in Genesis

Creation theology in Genesis shows much greater continuity with the ancient Near East, especially Mesopotamia, than is generally acknowledged. Ancient Israel shared a common culture with her neighbors which to a large extent shaped the literature of the Bible. For reasons not entirely clear to us the opening chapters of Genesis are typologically and content-wise more akin to the mythic traditions of Mesopotamia than of territorially closer Canaan—the reverse of the normal situation in the Hebrew Bible. In particular the so-called creation accounts in Genesis are clearly dependent upon the myths of ancient Mesopotamia and share with them fundamental assumptions about the divine and the human realms. A comparison of the two literatures reveals that they share greater continuity than discontinuity in fundamental assumptions about the deity, on the one hand, and about humankind and humankind's relationship to both deity and to the rest of creation, on the other hand.

There are differences, to be sure. But such differences are to be explained more from the exigencies of national theology and artistic license in composing an appropriate storyline congruent with Israel's theology than from a radically different understanding of deity and humankind. Even the impulse to develop a distinctive national theology, in the final analysis, stems from common cultural tendencies.

Elsewhere I have made the case that Israel's ancient theologians used myth and mythmaking speculation as one of their primary modes of theologizing. In this matter they were virtually indistinguishable from their ancient Near Eastern counterparts in Mesopotamia and Canaan,

16

save for the Yahwistic orientation of Israelite theological speculation.[1] In this article I wish to make explicit the essential continuity of thought between various "creation myths" of ancient Mesopotamia and the so-called primeval history of Genesis 1–9, which was implicit in my previous studies. This article builds upon the theses and evidence presented in those studies. The reader is advised to consult them for amplification and substantiation of numerous positions assumed here. The present article by design is more in the form of an essay which attempts broad conclusions rather than a detailed presentation of an entirely new thesis.

The approach adopted here is unabashedly diachronic, since that best reveals the lines of development from Mesopotamia through several layers of redaction in the primeval myth of Genesis. Without wishing to denigrate the advances in interpretation gained from synchronic approaches, only a diachronic reconstruction of Genesis 1–9, uncertain as that reconstruction may be at times, allows the reader to grasp the evolving emphasis in creation theology in Genesis from an earlier stage (the Yahwistic account or J, composed prior to 722 B.C.E.) to a later stage (the Priestly account or P, likely composed out of the experience of the Babylonian exile of the sixth century B.C.E.). I accept the thesis that P never existed as an independent narrative; rather P was written as a supplement to J and depends upon J to flesh out its narrative structure.[2] However, the priestly revision so radically altered the shape and meaning of the prior "Israelite epic" that P deserves to be called the author of the "Tetrateuch" (Genesis–Numbers) in its present form.

The primeval story in Genesis, especially the Yahwistic version, is explicitly set in the vicinity of Sumer (Shinar), suggesting a Mesopotamian source for its ideas. The biblical flood story has long been recognized as dependent upon prior Mesopotamian myth. The Mesopotamian roots of various Garden of Eden topoi—the creation of humankind from clay and divine spirit, the original nakedness of the human couple, the tree of life, the loss of immortality because of a serpent, and others—is only

1. See my *Slaying the Dragon: Mythmaking in the Biblical Tradition* (Louisville: Westminster/John Knox, 1992), especially chaps. 1–3; and a forthcoming article, "Paradise Reexamined," in *The Biblical Canon in Comparative Perspective: Scripture in Context IV* (ed. K. L. Younger, Jr., W. W. Hallo, and B. Batto; Lewiston/Queenston/Lampeter: Edwin Mellen, 1992), 33–66.

2. See, among others, F. M. Cross, *Canaanite Myth and Hebrew Epic* (Cambridge: Harvard University, 1973) 293–325.

slightly less patent. Accordingly, we begin our essay with a survey of Mesopotamian "creation theology."

The Mesopotamian Tradition

Mesopotamian literature is rich in texts which speak of the early stages of human history. Only a few of these may be classified as creation myths per se. More common are myth fragments and mythemes which are incorporated into other literary contexts (rituals, incantations, disputations, town or sanctuary etymologies, national myths, and the like). They are attested both for Sumerian literature (generally speaking, the earlier traditions) and for Akkadian literature (generally, the later traditions).

Two themes emerge as common to the whole of the Sumero-Akkadian tradition. (1) Humankind advanced in the course of history from a lesser to a higher state, aided by divine wisdom. (2) Humans, while possessing something of the divine spirit, are not divine but rather are servants of the gods. Each of these themes warrants fuller explication. To these may be added a third, subsidiary characteristic: increasingly in later periods creation myths were converted into national myths which served to undergird the hegemony of Babylon and Assyria, respectively.

1. The Advancement of Humankind

One of the constant themes in Mesopotamian literature is the advancement of humankind from a lower to a higher state. In the beginning humans were little more than animals. But thanks to various gifts from the gods, humankind gradually evolved, climaxing in the high civilizations of Sumer and Akkad. In Mesopotamian conception there was no "golden age" at the beginning of human history.

Although it has been asserted that the motif of a primeval paradise is attested in Sumerian literature,[3] a careful examination of the texts in question show that such is not the case.[4] Descriptions in the myth of

3. E.g., S. N. Kramer, *Enki and Ninhursag: A Sumerian 'Paradise' Myth* (BASOR SS 1; New Haven: ASOR, 1945) 8–9; idem, "The 'Babel of Tongues': A Sumerian Version," *JAOS* 88 (1968) 108–11. This interpretation as a paradise myth has been popularized through Kramer's translation of "Enki and Ninhursag" in *ANET*[3], 37–41, first published in 1950.

4. On the lack of an authentic paradise motif in Mesopotamian tradition and in early biblical tradition (J), see my article, "Paradise Reexamined." See also B. Alster, "Dilmun,

Enki and Ninhursag of "pure Dilmun" as a place where "the lion slew not, the wolf was not carrying off lambs"; where there was no eye-disease, no headache, no old woman, no old man, are not descriptions of a lost paradise in which animals did not prey upon one another or where illness and death were unknown. Rather such statements were intended to depict Dilmun before any form of life or civilization existed there. "There was no *x*, there was no *y*" was a common Sumerian literary formula for evoking "an initially inchoate world" before it received it final form, its present mode of being.[5]

In the Sumerian conception the primeval period of human history was far from paradisiacal. Primeval humans were barely distinguishable from animals. In the words of the myth of Ewe and Wheat (Lahar and Ashnan):

> The people of those distant days,
> They knew not cloth to wear;
> They went about with naked limbs in the land,
> And like sheep they ate grass with their mouth,
> Drinking water from the ditches.[6]

As the context makes clear, these are not depictions of an idyllic, pastoral world in which humankind and nature are in harmony. Rather they make a statement about the subhuman condition of humankind before humans learned to weave cloth and make garments, before they learned to till the ground and grow food. Other texts draw an even bleaker picture. According to The Rulers of Lagash primeval humans were dim-witted and completely at the mercy of the elements. In pens they bedded down on straw like cattle because they didn't know to build houses; they relied on what the rain produced on the steppes because they had not yet learned to till the soil or dig irrigation canals.[7] One could cite still other

Bahrain, and the Alleged Paradise in Sumerian Myth and Literature," in *Dilmun: New Studies in the Archaeology and Early History of Bahrain* (ed. D. Potts; BBVO 2; Berlin: Dietrich Reimer, 1983) 39–74.

5. T. Jacobsen, *The Harps That Once . . . : Sumerian Poetry in Translation* (New Haven and London: Yale University, 1987) 182. See also M. Jastrow, "Sumerian Myths of Beginnings," *AJSL* 33 (1916) 107; M. Lambert and R. Tournay, "Enki et Ninhursag," *RA* (1949) 105–36; P. Attinger, "Enki et Ninhursaga," *ZA* 74 (1984) 33–44.

6. For the most recent treatment of this text see B. Alster and H. Vanstiphout, "Lahar and Ashnan: Presentation and Analysis of a Sumerian Disputation," *Acta Sumerologica* 9 (1987) 1–43.

7. E. Sollberger, "The Rulers of Lagash," *JCS* 21 (1969) 279–91.

texts, e.g., UET 6. 61 ("The Eridu Genesis") which contains similar language.[8]

This is the context in which a second alleged Sumerian paradise text must be read also.[9] The text is the so-called "Babel of Tongues" passage—more exactly, "Nudimmud's spell"—in the epic Enmerkar and the Lord of Aratta.[10] This texts says that "in those days," there being no snakes, scorpions, hyenas, lions, dogs, or wolves—"nothing fearful or hair-raising"—humankind had nothing to fear. The Mardu (or "Westerners") were "lying in safe pastures." At that time the whole world still spoke but one language. Then the god of wisdom, Enki (traditionally the creator and patron of humankind), "changed the tongues in their mouths" so that they spoke many languages. While this may strike our romantic ears as the depiction of an idyllic place in which there was absolute harmony between beasts and humans, the Sumerians heard it quite differently. The Sumero-Akkadians took pride in being a "polyglot" people who could speak both Sumerian and Akkadian, and other languages besides. They gloried in their magnificent walled cities and despised barbarians like the "Westerners" who lived in tents in the open countryside.

Even the "harmony" between humans and beasts turns out on closer inspection to be a negative judgment on the conditions of the first humans. Civilization brought with it enmity between humankind and the beasts. The innovation of agricultural technology required the plowing up of the grazing ranges of the beasts. The domestication of animals meant that the tamed creatures must now be defended against their more ferocious cousins. Once humans abandoned their animalistic ways, they took to driving off and even killing the "wild beasts" which threatened their new way of life. Accordingly, the statement that humankind had nothing to fear from wild beasts can only mean that we are still in that primeval period when humans and animals were as yet barely distinguishable. The two species had not yet come into opposition.

These motifs are all recapitulated in the figure of Enkidu in the

8. See T. Jacobsen, "The Eridu Genesis," *JBL* 100 (1981) 513–29.

9. B. Alster, "An aspect of 'Enmerkar and the Lord of Aratta,'" *RA* 67 (1973) 101–9; Batto, "Paradise Reexamined," 42–50.

10. S. N. Kramer, *Enmerkar and the Lord of Aratta: A Sumerian Epic Tale of Iraq and Iran* (Philadelphia: Museum Monographs, 1952). A new edition was prepared by Sol Cohen, *Enmerkar and the Lord of Aratta* (Ph.D. Thesis; University of Pennsylvania, 1973). For a recent translation see T. Jacobsen, *The Harps That Once*, 275–319.

Gilgamesh epic. In his original state Enkidu was less than human; he was created a *lullû*, a word elsewhere reserved for primeval humankind. Enkidu is depicted as a virtual animal, shaggy and covered with hair over his entire body. In this "naked" condition he ranged over the steppes with the wild beasts and shared their ways, even to the extent of eating grass and drinking from the same watering hole. Then through intercourse with the harlot Shamhat, who served as much a midwife as a mate, Enkidu became a new being. From Shamhat Enkidu learned to wear clothes, and to drink water and to eat bread using his hands. In short, Enkidu "became human" (*awēliš iwē,* OB Gilg. II.iii.25; cf. *kīma muti ibašši* "he is like a human," 27). Moreover, when the *human* Enkidu attempted to return to his former ways, he discovered that he was no longer able to keep up with the wild beasts and, further, that the wild beasts no longer accepted him as one of them. His "harmony" with the beasts was gone. Although Enkidu at first lamented his "loss," Shamhat reassured him that he had actually gained. "You are beautiful, you have become like a god," she told him, for he had acquired wisdom (I.4.29), the gift of the gods. The final stage in Enkidu's humanization came when Shamhat led Enkidu to the walled city of Uruk and introduced him to Gilgamesh, that is, to urban society with its divinely instituted kingship.

Civilization was considered the crowning gift of the gods. The Sumerian King List speaks of kingship being lowered from heaven on successive city-states. A recently published, fragmentary Neo-Babylonian text is probably a composition about kingship being divinely created, as a sequel to the creation of humankind.[11] Other traditions speak of (seven, normally) semidivine sages known as *apkallu* who "administer the 'patterns' (*uṣurātu*) of heaven and earth.[12] The "patterns" are somewhat elusive of definition, but refer to the sum total of arts and sciences and the institutions by which civilized people live. The *apkallu* taught these "patterns" to humankind before the flood; supposedly there has been no substantial new knowledge since.

Even from this brief sketch it is clear that Mesopotamia lacked any notion of a golden age or of paradisiacal conditions at humankind's

11. W. R. Mayer, "Ein Mythos von der Erschaffung des Menschen und des Königs," *Or* 56 (1987) 55–68.

12. See J. Tigay, *The Evolution of the Gilgamesh Epic* (Philadelphia: University of Pennsylvania, 1982) 143 n. 8, and 205–6; W. G. Lambert, "Ancestors, Authors, and Canonicity," *JCS* 11 (1957) 1–14.

inception. Rather, Mesopotamian poets and theologians thought of human history in terms of growth or advancement. The complete definition of humankind came by stages. Primeval humans were scarcely more than animals. The ideal human condition was achieved only in (Sumero-Akkadian) civilization, with its advanced knowledge of irrigation agriculture, urban comforts, and justly famous literary tradition in both Sumerian and Akkadian, all organized under the leadership of a divinely appointed king.

2. Humans as Servants of the Gods

Evidence for the gradual definition of humankind, considered in the preceding section, had to be gleaned from a variety of texts of different genres. The theme of humans as servants of the gods is likewise attested in a variety of texts. However, this theme is epitomized in the Akkadian myth of Atrahasis.

Atrahasis is one of several great literary compositions written during the Old Babylonian period. During the Old Babylonian period Akkadian displaced Sumerian as the preferred literary vehicle. The translation of classical Sumerian tradition into the new "vernacular" was not slavishly done, however. Old Babylonian poets — should one say theologians? — took the opportunity to recompose the old traditions into new literary myths. J. Tigay has documented in great detail this process for the Gilgamesh tradition.[13] A similar genius was at work in the composition of the literary myth of Atrahasis. Although an entirely new composition, the older traditions resonated in it with such vibrancy that succeeding generations accepted it as their standard "creation myth."

Atrahasis has been called "the Babylonian flood story" by its modern editors.[14] More correctly, it is a myth of human origins, which incorporates an older Sumerian flood tradition. It defines the raison d'être of humankind and provides assurance for its continued existence. Fundamentally, humans were created to serve as substitute laborers for the gods, that is, to be the servants of the gods.

Before there was humankind, the gods had to provide their own food. With the model of Mesopotamian agricultural economy in mind, the

13. J. Tigay, *The Evolution of the Gilaamesh Epic.*

14. W. G. Lambert and A. R. Millard, *Atra-ḫasīs: The Babylonian Story of the Flood* (Oxford: Clarendon, 1969).

author says that in the beginning the high gods (Anunnaki) made the lesser gods (Igigi) plow the fields and dig the irrigation canals. When these lesser gods revolted, the high gods, under the leadership of Enlil their king, devised a plan to create substitute laborers so that the lesser gods also might enjoy godly rest. Wise Enki and the mother goddess teamed up to create primeval humans (*lullû*). Appropriately, they executed the ringleader of the rebel gods and from his blood mixed with clay they formed the new creatures. However, all Enki's wisdom was insufficient to anticipate the problems inherent in this course.

Along with the blood of the slain rebel god, these primeval humans had inherited his spirit (*eṭemmu*) and his tendency to scheme (*ṭēmu*). Soon similar noises of rebellion began to emerge from their midst. The more numerous these *lullû* became, the more threatening their noises became to the king of the gods; Enlil was unable to sleep. Like the rebellious deity from whom they were generated, these primeval humans aspired to divine status also. Their "cries" (*rigmu*), a replication of the "cries" of the rebel gods before them, are a metaphor for revolt against their ordained vocation and a challenging of divine sovereignty.[15]

Subsequent developments reveal clearly the inchoate character of the gods' initial attempt at creating humankind. The problem lay in the dual nature of primeval humankind. On the one hand, having been created out of the clay, humankind manifestly was linked with the earth and had much in common with the beasts of the earth. (Although not explicitly stated, *Atrahasis* assumes the common Mesopotamian view that animal-kind like humankind was created from clay.[16]) On the other hand, having been generated partially from a divine principle, humankind also shared a commonality with the gods. Their cries were of rebellion against their role as the gods' servants; they aspired to the status of divinity also.

King Enlil with his divine council sought to suppress this challenge to the divinely established order by decimating the ranks of the rebels

---

15. See B. Batto, "The Sleeping God: An Ancient Near Eastern Motif of Divine Sovereignty," *Bib* 68 (1987) 153–77.

16. The poem of Erra, which is dependent upon Atrahasis for the motif of humankind being almost obliterated because of its cries which disturb the deity, makes explicit what Atrahasis implies, namely the animals and humans alike were drawn from clay: "Let men be frightened and may their noise subside; may the herds (animalkind) shake and turn into clay again" (Erra 1:73–74; cf. IV.150); see L. Cagni, *The Poem of Erra* (Sources and Monographs: Sources from the Ancient Near East 1/3; Malibu, CA: Undena, 1977) 29 n. 19.

through plague, drought, and famine. When such means proved unsuccessful—thanks to Enki's benevolent intervention on behalf of his creatures—the gods decided to annihilate the entire earthly population through a universal flood. Meanwhile, Enki worked to preserve his handiwork and to secure an authentic place for humankind within the divine order.

In the end a solution to the dilemma was found through the creation of death. No thought had been given to the issue of mortality when primeval humankind was initially conceived. Endowed with the divine spirit, death was not automatic for primeval humankind. The divine assembly reassembled and instructed Enki to adjust his creation by imposing additional "patterns" or "regulations for people" (*uṣurāt nišī*) on these primeval humans, the principal of which was death.[17] The mortality of humankind was a central issue of Mesopotamian theology, as is evident from the prominence of this theme in other texts such as Adapa and Gilgamesh. Accordingly, with this adjustment primeval humankind (*lullû-amēlu*) came to an end and humankind as we know it (*amēlu*) came into being. The flood was the dividing point between the primeval age and the "present."

Furthermore, the principle was established that humankind should not be indiscriminately lumped together. In the parallel flood passage in Gilgamesh (XI.80), Enki reproached Enlil, "On the sinner lay his sin, on the transgressor lay his transgression." Atrahasis—identified as "king" in the Sumerian Flood Story—had been singular in his devotion to his patron deity Enki, which was apparently the reason for his selection as the flood hero and progenitor of postdiluvian humankind. Atrahasis confirmed his piety by immediately offering sacrifice to the gods upon disembarking from his ship at the conclusion of the flood.

In Atrahasis the creator god had found the model of what humankind should be, a mortal who accepted his position as servant of the gods, symbolized in his sacrificial offering of food to the gods. With the definition of humankind thus achieved, Enlil gave his blessing to these new mortals. The place of humankind in the divine order was now secure. The primeval period, the time of origins, thus came to its conclusion—and with it this myth of origins.

---

17. See W. G. Lambert, "The Theology of Death," in *Death in Mesopotamia* (ed. B. Alster; Mesopotamia 8; Copenhagen: Akademisk, 1980) 54–58.

3. The Conversion of Creation Myths into National Myths

From the very beginning of the literate period, and perhaps millennia before, myths have been used to validate the institutions of a society. In Mesopotamia myths had long been used to undergird the authority of sanctuaries and the hegemony of individual city-states. The Sumerian myth Enki and Ninhursag seems to have functioned in part as an etymology for both how Ninsikila became installed in her sanctuary and how Ensak came to be the patron deity of Dilmun. The Sumerian myth Enmerkar and the Lord of Aratta claims that Inanna favored Kulab, and so provided justification for the prominence of that sanctuary and of the city of Uruk which encompassed it. Other examples could be cited. Nonetheless, the tendency to use myths for political propaganda reached a new plateau with the rise of the nation-states of Babylon and Assyria.

The most blatant example is the "creation myth" Enuma elish, a specifically Babylonian version of the Semitic Combat Myth in which the patron deity of Babylon defeated the watery chaos dragon en route to becoming the divine sovereign of heaven and earth. This myth patently was composed to justify Babylon's rise from a previously insignificant city to hegemony over the whole of Mesopotamia. Somewhat earlier the Akkadian myth of Anzu, upon which Enuma elish is partially patterned, had attempted to stake out a similar claim for the city of Girsu in central Mesopotamia by having its patron deity Ninurta defeat the demonic Anzu after the older gods proved unequal to the task. Similarly, Enuma elish tells how an older hierarchy of gods was first established but then became inadequate when faced with the ultimate challenge of slaying the chaos dragon Tiamat, necessitating the transfer of authority to a younger and more vigorous deity, Marduk.

Enuma elish is more of a theogony than a cosmogony; it is more concerned with the origins of the gods and the hierarchy among them than with the establishment of the world and the origins of humankind. Nevertheless, it incorporates elements of cosmogony from Atrahasis. After Marduk defeated Tiamat, he fashioned the cosmos from her body. Then, stealing a page from Atrahasis, Marduk created humankind so that all the gods might have rest. Faithful to the older myth, humankind was molded from a mixture of clay and the blood of the slain leader of the rebel gods, in this case Qingu, husband of Tiamat. Enuma elish bows to the authority of Atrahasis by retaining Enki as the deity who physically fashioned humankind, but portrays Enki as merely carrying out the designs of Marduk, the mastermind of the plan.

The author of Enuma elish intended this new composition to supplant the older myth as the authentic cosmogony. If Atrahasis opened in primeval time when the gods had to raise their own food because humans had not yet been thought up, Enuma elish claims to go back even before that time, before the gods themselves had been generated. By such strategy the author sought to establish Enuma elish as the ultimate theological statement. Just as the position of preeminence among the gods was claimed for Marduk, so precedence among myths was claimed for the myth which narrates Marduk's ascendancy as the divine sovereign.

But if Babylon could manipulate myth as national political propaganda, so could Assyria. When Enuma elish reached Assyria, Assyrian editors replaced the name of Marduk with that of their own national deity, Ashur. Instead of undergirding Babylonian hegemony, the revised Enuma elish supported Assyrian hegemony over Babylon!

The Yahwistic Primeval Myth

With justification J has been regarded as an early, if not the earliest version of "the Israelite epic." Implicit in this description is an acknowledgement that J functioned as a national epic, similar to the national epics of other ancient Near Eastern nations. Whether J was written to provide a national theology for the Davidic kingdom is a moot question. But certainly J makes the claim that Israel is the most blessed of nations because of her election by Yahweh, an election sealed through her unique covenant with the deity. Again, although not monotheistic in its claims, J sets forth the thesis that Israel's god Yahweh is the creator and by implication the head of the pantheon. Indeed, the other gods are reduced to shadowy, functionless figures (Gen 3:22 [cf. 3:5]; 6:1–4; 11:7).

The Yahwist's primeval myth is to be found in the J portions of Genesis 2–8, i.e., the stories of Eden, Cain and Abel, and Lamech (2:4–4:26), and the flood (6:1–8:22 [here J and P are intertwined]). Like the Babylonian myth of Atrahasis, the Yahwist's primeval myth ended with the conclusion of the flood. Indeed, as I have demonstrated elsewhere, the Yahwist patterned his[18] primeval myth upon Atrahasis. To bridge the time

18. The masculine pronoun is used here on the assumption that the scribal profession

between the conclusion of the primeval period and the beginning of "Israelite history" with the patriarchs (Genesis 12), J added another period, the "world history" (now found within Genesis 9–11).[19]

Although the Yahwist's myth cannot be reduced to a single theme, the primary focus is on the definition of humankind, including humankind's role in relation to deity and to the rest of creation. On the one side, humankind bears some commonality with animals, but is more than an animal. On the other side, humankind also possesses something of the divine spirit, but is not truly divine. Like other ancient Near Eastern "creation" myths, the Yahwist's primeval myth is about defining humankind and grounding the world of humankind within a divinely established order.

The common interpretation of Genesis 2–3 as the story of "the Fall" must be discarded as inconsistent with the Yahwist's purpose and meaning. Implicit in the idea of a "Fall" is the belief that Eden was a paradise, an idyllic place created for the enjoyment of humankind, where there was neither sickness nor death, and where there was absolute harmony between deity and humankind and between humankind and the rest of creation. The very first point to be made is that the Yahwist's creation story was not a paradise story. It goes without saying that J could not have been based on a Mesopotamian paradise myth, as frequently alleged, because as noted earlier Mesopotamia lacked an authentic primeval paradise motif. Rather than being the story of humankind's fall from a higher to a lower state, the Yahwist's primeval myth is the story of a continuously improved creation, which reached its culmination in the final definition of humankind at the conclusion of the flood in Genesis 8.

Like Atrahasis, the Yahwist assumes the setting for the creation of humankind to have been a barren wasteland in the region of Mesopotamia, before there was any rain or rivers to make the ground fertile. There Yahweh God planted a garden and irrigated it with rivers originating in the underworld. Then Yahweh formed a solitary primeval human

---

was a male dominated profession. However, there is nothing to preclude the possibility of the Yahwist having been a woman, as noted by R. Friedman (*Who Wrote the Bible?* [New York: Summit Books, 1987] 85–86). In any case Harold Bloom (*The Book of J* [Grove: Weidenfeld, 1990]) exceeds the meager biblical evidence in pinpointing J as a royal woman in the court of Rehoboam.

19. W. M. Clark, "The Flood and the Structure of the Pre-patriarch History," *ZAW* 83 (1971) 184–211.

(*hā'ādām*) from the earth/soil (*hā-'ădāmâ*), whose function was to cultivate the garden and to care for it (2:15).

What is usually missed in the Eden story is that Yahweh was the original gardener. It was he "planted" the garden and made to grow there all kinds of beautiful shrubbery and delicious fruit trees, including the two mythic, divine trees: "the tree of life" and "the tree of knowledge of good and evil" (2:8–9). He was also the original irrigator. The garden was a fabulous place, the deity's private preserve (cf. "the garden of God," Ezek 28:13), where he liked to walk in the refreshing afternoon breeze (3:8). The primeval human was created to work the garden (2:5,8,15), apparently to relieve the deity—or perhaps better, the gods[20]—from the agricultural chores of providing food for the divine realm, much as in Atrahasis.

This linkage to the soil seems to provide the explanation for Cain's sin. When humankind was expelled from the garden, it carried with it the divine decree "to labor at the soil from which it was taken" (3:23). Cain was just such "a laborer of the soil" (4:2). Without going into detail, the narrator informs us that Cain's offering was unacceptable to Yahweh. In keeping with Cain's character of breaking the bond with the soil, Cain brought further curse upon the soil by spilling his brother's blood upon it. As a result, the rift between humankind and soil—and at the same time between the creator and humankind—is widened (4:12–14,16).

In Eden humankind had permission to eat the produce of the garden; the fruit of the tree of knowledge was expressly forbidden, however. Apparently the fruit of this tree was wisdom, since eating it made the humans wise like gods (3:5; 3:22). The idea of a wisdom tree seems to have sprouted from the Yahwist's own fertile imagination; nevertheless, his imagination may have been fired here by themes from Atrahasis as well. It was the wisdom god Enki who created humankind. The name Atrahasis (Enki's devotee) means "the extra-wise one." In Mesopotamia wisdom was a divine trait which was given to humankind, for example, by semi-divine sages, the *apkallu*. The attempt to restrict wisdom from humankind was for the Yahwist apparently a metaphor for the distinction between deity and humankind. As in Atrahasis, humankind over-reached the boundary between deity and humankind and grasped at divinity. The text says that the eyes of the humans were opened by their

---

20. Note that "like gods" (3:5) is later rephrased "like one of *us*" (3:21). Note also "the sons of God" (*or* "the sons of the gods"; 6:1); cf. "let *us* go down" (11:7).

eating of the fruit; but Yahweh's eyes were opened as well. He realized that humankind would continue to grasp at divinity, so he drove them out of the garden, lest they further trespass the boundary between human and divine by eating also of the tree of life and become immortal as well (3:22).

Like Enlil and Enki, Yahweh was naive about his creation. Molded from clay and animated from the deity's own breath, earth matter and divine spirit, humankind was from the first ill-conceived on several accounts. The first mistake to become apparent was the creating of but a solitary being. To solve this first creature's loneliness Yahweh molded additional creatures, all kinds of animals, from clay as well. When this tactic proved unsuccessful, the deity redid the primeval human by dividing it into male and female. But the question still remained about the relation of animalkind and humankind. They shared a common earthly origin. Moreover, the first humans were naked, just as the animals. They were also ignorant, apparently, much as the animals. Only as the narrative progresses is the difference between animals and humans clarified. As humans acquired wisdom, that is, became more god-like, they began to wear clothes, the symbol of a distinctive humanness. But even then Yahweh made sure that they were clothed in skin garments, perhaps to remind the humans that they still retained a kinship with the animals.

Humankind acquired wisdom but not by divine design. Begrudgingly the deity had to admit that with the acquisition of wisdom humankind had "become like gods," seemingly an acknowledgment that humankind may be closer in nature to deity than to animalkind.

Were these humans divine, then? They did not have divine blood coursing through their veins, as the *lullû* in Atrahasis; but primeval humankind was animated by the deity's own breath. The definition of *'ădām* as a creature of and for the earth/soil (*'ădāmâ*) was in danger of being lost. Even denying humankind access to the tree of life did not fully solve this problem.[21] Primeval humankind's vitality continued largely

---

21. At this point J is perhaps closer to Gilgamesh and Adapa than to Atrahasis. Like "Adam," "Adapa" means "Man/Human" (A.DA.AB=*a-mi-lu; MSL* XII, 93); Adapa is addressed as "Man" (*amīlu;* Adapa B,21). Adapa lost the opportunity for immortality when at the advice of wise Enki/Ea, patron deity and creator of humankind, Adapa declined to eat the bread of life and the water of life offered him by Anu, king of the gods. Whether the wisdom deity misled Adapa inadvertently or by design is unclear. Given the common ancient Near Eastern motif of denial of immortality to humans, one suspects that Enki

unabated, as the extraordinarily long life spans of the antediluvians indicated. Again as in Atrahasis, the growing numbers of humans proved a threat to the deity (6:1–4), eventually provoking Yahweh to blot the whole population off the face of the earth with a universal flood.

One frequently encounters the assertion that the biblical flood story bears only superficial resemblance to the Mesopotamian account.[22] Such judgments are now completely antiquated, having been formulated when our primary witness to the Mesopotamian flood story was the truncated version found in tablet XI of the Gilgamesh myth. In Gilgamesh the flood account was introduced only secondarily, as an example of how difficult it is for even the most extraordinary of humans to attain immortality, something that rightly belongs the divinities alone. With the recovery of the Atrahasis myth we are compelled to recognize just how dependent the Yahwist was upon Mesopotamian antecedents. Both Atrahasis and the Yahwistic primeval myth place the flood in the context of a primeval humankind's refusal to accept its servant role, grasping at divinity instead. In both accounts the flood is unleashed as "divine retribution" for that "sin." In both accounts a pious ("righteous") hero is saved to begin a new generation of humans. In both accounts the flood hero offers acceptable sacrifice which appeases the deity. In both accounts a divine sign is given guaranteeing a secure place for humankind within a divinely established order, effectively concluding the primeval period.

The sending of the flood itself was an implicit admission of original failure on the part of the creator. The experiment did not work as expected. Yahweh "regretted" having made humankind and so determined to blot it off the face of the earth along with all the other creatures, "(everything) from humankind to the beasts to the creeping things and even the birds of the sky; for I regret that I made them!" (6:7). This decision is contradicted in the very next verse, however, for the creator determined to spare Noah and a representative portion of every kind of living creature

intended that immortality should be denied to Adapa, the representative of humankind. There is also evidence that Adapa and Atrahasis are essentially the same character; see B. Batto, *Slaying the Dragon,* chap. 1, n. 23.

22. For a recent example, see the note in *NRSV* at Gen 6:7: "The biblical account is superficially similar to the Babylonian Gilgamesh Epic, which also relates the story of a great flood. The biblical perspective, however, is basically different, for the flood was not the expression of a polytheistic caprice but of God's judgment upon *the wickedness of humankind.*"

because Noah "found favor in Yahweh's eyes" (6:8). In Atrahasis the decision to send the flood and the decision to rescue a remnant of humankind proceeded from two distinct divine parties, represented by Enlil and by Enki, respectively. The Yahwist was forced to attribute both actions to Yahweh, since in his theology Yahweh is the only deity with real authority.

As was the case in Atrahasis, the Yahwist's postdiluvian humankind was an entirely different species from antediluvian humankind. Though death was known in the antediluvian period, it was not regularized. At the flood Yahweh imposed a limit upon human vitality at one hundred and twenty years (6:3). Human mortality was now defined clearly by divine decree.

Fittingly, the postdiluvian world was repopulated from the descendants of the flood hero. The flood hero, whether in Mesopotamia or in Israel, was a model of what humankind should be. Atrahasis was a model of obedience to Enki; in the Sumerian Flood Story he even lives in the deity's temple, apparently as a priest of Enki.[23] Noah alone of all his generation "found favor in Yahweh's eyes" (Gen 6:8; cf. P: "Noah was a righteous man, perfect in his generation," 6:9). Atrahasis's first act upon disembarking from his boat was to sacrifice to the gods. In the context of a myth in which humans were created to do the agricultural work of the gods, this can only mean that he has accepted his servant role of feeding the gods. Similarly, Noah's sacrifice functions as a signal that he has accepted the task of humankind as cultivator of the soil. Yahweh's response to the sacrifice is a retraction of his curse upon the ground uttered in the garden (8:21; cf. 3:17–19; 4:10–14). After the flood Noah is characterized as "the man of the soil" and his only recorded activity in the postdiluvian world is agricultural (9:20), thus fulfilling the prophecy at his birth that he would bring relief from the curse upon the soil (5:29).

The Priestly Revision of the Primeval Myth

The Yahwist's primeval story is no more. The Priestly Writer, writing several hundred years after the Yahwist, in the shadow of the Babylonian exile, found the Yahwist's primeval myth less than satisfactory for his day and set about salvaging it by a thorough rewriting. Apparently the

23. See R. Borger, "Notes brèves: 10. Sur le récit de Déluge RS 22421," *RA* 64 (1970) 189.

Yahwistic account was by now too well entrenched in Israelite tradition to be ignored. In any case the Priestly Writer placed the old Yahwistic account within a new frame of his own making.[24] In this new frame the primeval story acquired an entirely different look and meaning.

The Priestly Writer was unhappy with the Yahwistic primeval story for several reasons. One of the most important was the unflattering portrait of the deity. Yahweh God appeared to be not merely naive but even bumbling in his efforts at creation. He required several attempts before he was able to come up with a workable model for humankind. Even, then Yahweh God appeared to be less in control of his universe than merely reacting to situations which challenged his authority. (Such images of the deity could scarcely have inspired confidence within an exilic Israelite community, still in shock over their world being turned topsy-turvy by the superior, infidel Babylonian empire.) One of P's goals was to repaint the portrait of the Creator as the divine sovereign who not only did everything right the first time, but who also had the universe firmly under control. This he did by two strategies. First, through a series of artful insertions inspired in part by the Babylonian myth of Enuma elish, P recast the whole primeval myth as scene in the divine sovereign's battle to overcome the chaos dragon. Second, he prefaced the whole of the primeval story with his own version of "creation" in which God is shown to have created everything perfect.

1. Creation as a Combat Myth

If the Yahwist patterned his primeval myth principally on Atrahasis, the Priestly Writer seemingly found in the Babylonian version of the Combat Myth, Enuma elish, a more appropriate model for God. Combat Myth motifs may not be as explicit in Genesis as elsewhere in the Bible,[25] but they are nonetheless present in many vestigial forms.[26] The fact that the P account begins not with a dry wasteland but with the watery Abyss (*těhōm*), is the first indication that we are operating within the context of the Combat Myth. The Abyss may be less personified than Tiamat

24. Within the primeval story the following passages are to be assigned to P: Gen 1:1–2:4a; 5:1–33 (except v 29); 6:9–22; 7:11,13–16a,17a,18–21–24; 8:1–2a,3b–5,14–19; 9:1–17.

25. E.g., Isa 27:1; 51:9–11; Jer 31:35; Job 26:12–13; Pss 74:10–17; 89:9–10.

26. See my book, *Slaying the Dragon*, chap. 3.

in Enuma elish or Yamm in the Canaanite Baal cycle, but it is nonetheless a force which must be subdued in order for the Creator's design to come into being. Like Tiamat's body, the Abyss is divided into two, above and below, in order to make space for the ordered "world." The image of living within a "bubble," surrounded on all sides by the nihilistic powers of chaos, appropriately evoked images of the precariousness of existence. Creation would cease in an instant, were the divine sovereign not in his heaven keeping the chaos dragon in submission.

The scene of God resting at the completion of his work of creation was a signal that the Creator did indeed have everything under control. In the ancient Near East divine "rest" was a metaphor for the correct order.[27] The theme of the rest, or sleep, of the gods is prominent in Atrahasis. The rebel gods, and later rebellious humankind, disturbed the sleep of Enlil. Disturbing the divine sovereign's sleep was tantamount to challenging his authority. In the end the rebel gods got to rest as well, symbolic of their having attained their proper status as gods. In Enuma elish this same scene is retold with Marduk as the one who created humankind "so that the gods may have rest" (En. el. VI.8,36,131). The theme of the divine sovereign resting is prominent also in Enuma elish. Early in the myth Ea (Enki) defeated the husband of Tiamat and, after crowning himself in Apsu's stead, retired to his palace to rest (En. el. I.75). Later, when Ea proved inadequate to face Tiamat herself, Ea's son Marduk took up the challenge. Marduk too "rested" after his victory over Tiamat, from whose body he fashioned the world (IV.133–36). The building of his palace (temple) Esagila as a place of rest for all the gods (VI.121–130; VII.51–59) was an apt symbol of his unchallenged sovereignty, as was his hanging up of his no-longer-needed warbow in the sky (VI.82–90).

The Priestly Writer's audience no doubt also heard in Gen 1:1–2:3 echoes of the conflict between the chaos dragon and the divine sovereign. The rest of God at the conclusion would have been heard as reassurance that the god of Israel was indeed the universal divine sovereign — and not their conqueror's god, Marduk. God was in his heaven and has the world firmly in control. Nevertheless, in this priestly retelling, it is still too soon for the divine sovereign to retire his bow.

27. See B. Batto, "The Sleeping God: An Ancient Near Eastern Motif of Divine Sovereignty," *Bib* 68 (1987) 153–77.

The chaos dragon has seven heads according to Near Eastern myth. Although it has been slain once, it always seems to have yet another ugly head with which to wreak havoc on good order. This perpetual struggle lies behind the Egyptian text known as the "the Repulsing of the Dragon"; each day the sun god Re arose anew from the primeval ocean Nun to repulse Apophis, because it is an ongoing task to dispel darkness and chaos from our world. In Neo-Babylonian times at least, at the New Year Festival Babylonian priests ritually recited Enuma elish, perhaps as an annual renewal of Marduk's victory over Tiamat. Just such a prayer to Marduk to continue vanquishing Tiamat "until the last days of human-kind" is found in Marduk's forty-ninth title (VII.132–34). For his part, the Priestly Writer suggests that the flood and the victory over Pharaoh at the Red Sea were further instances of the chaos dragon attempting to challenge the divine sovereign.[28] Like other biblical writers writing out of the debacle of the Babylonian exile, by such images the Priestly Writer intended to offer hope to discouraged Israelites that Israel's god is the divine sovereign who slays the chaos dragon whenever and wherever it reappears: what he did to Pharaoh and his Egyptian hosts, he will do again to their infidel Babylonian masters.

2. A Perfect Creation

Babylonian theologians blatantly claimed for Marduk titles and func-tions which previously had been attributed to other gods.[29] The author of Enuma elish, as previously noted, made Marduk the real creator of humankind by reducing Enki to a mere craftsman carrying out Marduk's "artful designs." By a mere word Marduk could make things disappear and reappear, i.e., call things into existence or, vice-versa, cause them to cease existence.

The Priestly Writer found in this divine sovereign scene the model he needed for transforming the unsatisfactory Yahwistic portrait of a naive and inexperienced creator into that of an omnipotent and omniscient

28. See B. Batto, "The Reed Sea: *Requiescat in Pace*," *JBL* 102 (1983) 27–35; "Red Sea or Reed Sea?," *BARev* 10/4 (July/August 1984) 57–63.

29. See W. G. Lambert, "The Historical Development of the Mesopotamian Pantheon: A Study in Sophisticated Polytheism," in *Unity and Diversity: Essays in the History, Literature, and Religion of the Ancient Near East* (ed. Hans Goedicke and J. J. M. Roberts; Baltimore and London; Johns Hopkins University, 1975) 191–200, esp. 193–94.

Creator. This P was accomplished by prefacing the Yahwist's with a prior scene (Gen 1:1–2:3) which tells how the Creator tamed the Abyss and then brought into existence everything that is according to a well-conceived, orderly scheme. At each step along the way the Creator paused to survey his work, making sure that everything he had done was "good" (*kî ṭôb*). At the end the whole grand design was pronounced "perfect!" (*kî ṭôb mĕ'ōd*).

The author omitted the *kî ṭôb* formula from the descriptions of creation both of the firmament and of humankind, despite the latter being created "in the image and likeness of God." These omissions seem to be a case of deliberate foreshadowing. In the priestly reworking of the flood story, the onset of the flood was caused by a rupture in the firmament which allowed the Abyss temporarily to overwhelm the Creator's work. The divine sovereign had to repulse the Abyss once more and repair the firmament.

The case of humankind is more complex. The P passages leading up to the flood contain no stories of humans sinning, only the judgment in 6:11–13 that "all flesh has corrupted its way." By corrupt ways P apparently has reference to the old Yahwistic scenes of human rebellion ("Adam" and Eve, Cain and Abel, Lamech, the intercourse of the sons of God with the human daughters) — clear evidence that P intended his own writing and the older Yahwistic myth to be read as a single, unified composition. Even though created "in the image and likeness of God," humankind was not pronounced "good." It was because of human sin that the divine sovereign's archenemy, Abyss, was able to regain entry into God's "perfect" world and nearly undo it.

P's motive for departing from the pattern of Enuma elish in the matter of the bow has become clearer now. In the Babylonian myth the divine sovereign retired his bow upon the clouds at the conclusion of his battle with Tiamat. On that pattern the bow scene should have come at the end of Genesis 1. That, however, was manifestly inappropriate within the priestly scheme. P had to contend with the effects of including the Yahwist's epic into his composition. According to a long-standing tradition, the reconciliation between deity and humankind which transpired at the conclusion of the flood was guaranteed for some sign; in P's retelling of the story the bow serves that function.[30]

30. See B. F. Batto, "The Covenant of Peace: A Neglected Ancient Near Eastern Motif," *CBQ* 49 (1987) 187–211.

Even so, in P's vision the bow does double duty, for it also retains its symbolism as the weapon by which the divine sovereign defeated the chaos dragon. P made the flood into a recrudescence of the nihilistic force of Abyss. This time, however, Abyss was aided by rebellious humankind. In priestly theology Abyss is the personification of evil; but evil in turn is incarnated in history through human wickedness. Consequently, by postponing the retirement of the divine sovereign's bow until after the flood, P made the point that God does not allow chaos—evil, whether human or demonic, historical or metahistorical—to undo permanently the good order of his creation. The rainbow (God's warbow) in the clouds is also symbolic of God's pledge to maintain his sovereignty over creation.

The genius of the Priestly Writer is clearly evident. He was able to retain the older Israelite myth and yet give an entirely new theological "spin" to it. As composed by the Yahwist, the primeval myth had been a story of an original inchoate creation by an inexperienced and naive creator which was continuously improved until eventually an acceptable definition of humankind was achieved. But when viewed within its new Priestly frame, the primeval myth was transformed into a story of an originally perfect creation become corrupt through human sin.

At this point we find that the paradise issue has reentered the scene through a back door. In the myth penned by the Yahwist the garden of Eden was the deity's private preserve, not a paradise for humankind. But when viewed within its Priestly frame, Eden is transformed into an idyllic place. The aura of perfection from Genesis 1 spills over into Genesis 2. The image of humankind created in the image and likeness of God in Genesis 1 acts as a colored lens filtering out the servant aspect, but leaving humankind in the garden to indulge in its delectable fruits and presumably to enjoy Yahweh's company as he took his afternoon strolls in the refreshing shade of the garden. Only in Genesis 3, with the cursing of the human, his wife, and the ground, does the aura of perfection comes to an abrupt end. Under the pen of P the Eden story has become something of a "fall" after all.

Conclusion

For reasons we do not yet fully understand, the narratives in Genesis 1–11 reveal greater continuity with the Mesopotamian mythic tradition than with that of nearby Canaan. In its present form the Israelite primeval myth (Genesis 1–9) is a combination of an original Yahwistic primeval myth and later Priestly supplementation. J and P both drew heavily upon Mesopotamian cosmogonic tradition, even while creating a new and distinctively Israelite myth based on Yahwistic beliefs. J, being the first and lacking prior Israelite models, patterned his myth to a large extent upon the Akkadian cosmogonic myth Atrahasis, both with regard to structure and themes. P, attempting to maintain continuity with the tradition established by J even while reforming it, was more subtle in the manner in which he drew upon Mesopotamian myth, principally the Babylonian myth Enuma elish.

Like Atrahasis, the Yahwist's primeval myth establishes a secure ground for humankind within a divinely ordained order. It is a myth of inchoate beginnings; only through experimentation do both the creator and humankind discover humankind's authentic role as a species unto themselves, somewhere between animalkind and deity. By the end of the myth the character of humankind has been defined: mortal, created for divine service, but prone to overreach its true vocation by grasping at divine prerogatives. Nevertheless, in the end the deity is reconciled to an imperfect humankind and guarantees its place in the created order. If one looks beyond the primeval story, it is evident that the Yahwist was laying the ground for the election of Israel in the latter part of his composition. Despite Israel's continuous rebellion against Yahweh, Yahweh nonetheless bound himself in covenant to Israel as his elect people.

The two characteristic themes of Mesopotamian primeval theology make their appearance in the Yahwist's primeval myth as well: (1) The history of primeval humankind was one of progression. The tradition of primeval humankind being near-animals is present in vestigial form. Also, the end condition of humans possessing divine wisdom is prominent, though in modified form. (2) The theme of humankind as mortal divine servant forms the core of the Yahwistic narrative, as I have presented it. The third characteristic, the tendency to use primeval myths as religio-political propaganda, is less obvious in the Yahwist's primeval myth proper; but it will become central in later chapters of the Yahwist's composition.

Writing some centuries later and out of a totally different situation, the Priestly Writer sought to reform the Yahwist's myth, not to replace it. His primary goal was to maintain continuity with Israel's traditional faith, even while slanting it towards new concerns. Whether partly to combat Babylon's religio-political propaganda, or simply because of theological utility, P recast Israel's God as the universal divine sovereign using motifs borrowed from Enuma elish. P's borrowings are more subtle than J's, since he had to work around a preexisting narrative established by J. The results were dramatic, nonetheless, especially for the portrait of Israel's God. Instead of appearing as a naive and inexperienced creator, Yahweh was now recognizable as the omniscient and omnipotent sovereign of heaven and earth, whose authority no power in heaven, on earth, or under the earth can withstand. Evil can never overthrow the good order he has decreed, despite present appearances to the contrary. Like Deutero-Isaiah, P's was a message for discouraged exiles: the omnipotent and omniscient divine sovereign whose word keeps all creation eternally in order is the same deity who has promised to maintain an everlasting covenant with his elect people.

Though P's product had a quite different look about it, P pursued much the same method and goal as J—and ultimately Mesopotamia's theologians. P sought to ground his community's experience and its future in a creation theology. Our world is secure because God established it thus in primeval events.

In seeking a theology of creation, Israel's theologians used the culturally conditioned theological medium of their day: myth. Perhaps the real lesson here is not that Israelite theologians used the cultural myths of their day to convey their most profound understanding of humankind and deity, but that we have that failed to appreciate the theological profundity of ancient Near Eastern theologians generally.

ROBERT A. DI VITO

The Demarcation of Divine
and Human Realms
in Genesis 2–11

I. Introduction

If there have been in times past serious reservations about the aptness
of comparisons between the Yahwist's narrative of "Primeval History"
(PH) in Genesis 2:4b–11:26 and Sumerian and Akkadian literary texts,
the Lambert-Millard edition of Atrahasis seems to have finally put them
aside.[1] Whether one conceives of a direct or an indirect relationship
between the two traditions, biblical scholars now routinely acknowledge
the bearing of Mesopotamian traditions on the biblical text, and Sumerian
and Akkadian parallels figure into the interpretation of the Genesis narrative in increasingly significant ways. Given the antiquity, the variety,
and the sheer extent of Mesopotamia's literary legacy, this is surely a
welcome development; its benefits for biblical scholarship are already
apparent. The isolation of Genesis 2–3 within the Primeval History has
now largely disappeared; and, with renewed attention to chaps. 4–11,
the structural and thematic significance of the Flood within the PH has
come to light. The tendency now is to emphasize the ways in which the
biblical narrative and the works of ancient Mesopotamia manifest structural and thematic similarities.[2] Atrahasis, of course, has been particularly

1. W. G. Lambert and A. R. Millard, *Atra-ḫasīs: The Babylonian Story of the Flood*
(Oxford: Clarendon, 1969). All references are to this edition.
2. See in this volume, for example, the contribution by B. Batto.

prominent in this regard, and since the publication of Lambert and Millard, it is not uncommon to find scholars asserting that Atrahasis and the PH have similar, if not identical, plots.[3]

There are certainly significant differences among these researchers, but a number hold in common a conviction about the Bible's theme, which is supported by appeal to Atrahasis. This is the conviction that Genesis 2–11, directly or indirectly influenced by the paradigm of Atrahasis, articulates a fundamental separation, or distinction, between the divine and the human. This demarcation of divine and human spheres is entirely, or in large part, the outcome of multiple attempts by humanity to violate and, in fact, to obliterate a distinction between humanity and God, and to nullify the bounds which properly exist between the deity and human-kind. Out of these attempts by humans and the limitations or punish-ments these incur from the gods, the world as we know it is born. R. Oden's conclusion may be taken as typical of this approach: the message of both Atrahasis and the PH is "the divinely ordained separation of heaven and earth as two distinct realms, and the enforcement of distinct limits upon the human race."[4] Or, as W. M. Clark has put it, in Israel "any effort to achieve contact with the realm of the divine was strictly forbidden."[5]

If this is so, the consequences for an anthropology which would base itself upon the biblical narrative are obvious. In fact, one may suspect that such an interpretation of the PH may itself derive, at least in part, from a theological anthropology in which an absolute distinction of

3. So, e.g., R. J. Clifford, "Creation in the Hebrew Bible," *Physics, Philosophy, and Theology: A Common Quest for Understanding* (ed. R. J. Russell, W. R. Stoeger, S.J., and G. V. Coyne, S.J.; Vatican City: Vatican Observatory, 1988) 154. D. Damrosch (*The Narrative Covenant: Transformations of Genre in the Growth of Biblical Literature* [San Francisco: Harper & Row, 1987] 90–93, 118–35) for his part sees both the Genesis text and Gilgamesh in relation to what he calls the "creation-flood epic" genre (extant, for example, in Atrahasis) and focuses on the similarities between Gilgamesh and the Genesis narrative.

4. R. A. Oden, Jr. ("Divine Aspirations in Atrahasis and in Genesis 1–11," *ZAW* 93 [1981] 215–16), quoting P. D. Hanson's summary of the Yahwist's message in "Rebellion in Heaven, Azazel, and Euhemeristic Heroes in 1 Enoch 6–11," *JBL* 96 (1977) 214.

5. W. M. Clark, "The Flood and the Structure of the Pre-patriarchal History," *ZAW* 83 (1971) 192.

humankind and deity is fundamental. After all, there is reason to think that such an absolute distinction of the divine and the human is not nearly as decisive for the Bible or for the ancient Near East as is generally assumed in these interpretations. Here we only have to call attention to the important work of B. Albrektson, who has capably argued not only for the continuity of biblical and ancient Near Eastern historical thinking but also for the lack of any fundamental demarcation in that thought between the world of the gods and the world of human historical existence.[6] This is not, of course, to deny that there is a distinction between the gods and humans, or even to deny the importance of this distinction to ancient Near Eastern thinking (cf. Gilgamesh). Rather, it is a question of its decisiveness and, especially, of its thematic importance in the Yahwist's understanding of human cultural history.

It is the thesis of this paper that there is no divinely ordained separation of heaven and earth as two fundamentally distinct realms in the Yahwist's PH, nor does the world it describes emerge from repeated attempts by humans to trespass upon the divine sphere. This will be demonstrated by critically examining three texts of J's narrative in Genesis 2–11 where the demarcation of the human and divine realms is most frequently seen to be central to the text's interpretation. In each case, it will be shown that a viable interpretation of the narrative does not turn upon the infringement of ontological boundaries by humans as interpreters frequently assume. Consequently, such a demarcation of ontological territories cannot be the theme which dominates the PH as a whole (even as we would not see it to be crucial in Atrahasis). Furthermore, such a demarcation is not even viable in the attenuated form it assumes in Westermann's notion of the Yahwist "secularization" of human culture and cultural institutions in Genesis 2–11. The hermeneutical significance of Atrahasis, and of the Mesopotamian epic tradition generally, points in a different direction. Here direct comparisons highlight the significance of fundamentally different evaluations of human culture and the achievements of civilization. And it is this almost polemical reversal of Mesopotamia's endorsement of cultural institutions and achievements which is necessary to the comprehension of the Yahwist's work in the PH.

6. B. Albrektson, *History and the Gods: An Essay on the Idea of Historical Events as Divine Manifestations in the Ancient Near East and Israel* (Lund: Gleerup, 1967), chap. 4.

II. Primeval History as the Delineation
of the Ontological Difference
Between Humankind and Deity

For Oden, whom we take as representative of the position of a number of scholars,[7] the primary theme of both Atrahasis and the PH is "the development and maintenance of the boundary between the gods and humans" in view of the human tendency to "over-reach its limits" and "to encroach upon divine territory."[8] The aspiration for divine status, of course, provokes in each case a devastating punishment, namely the Flood, which almost completely destroys humanity. In Atrahasis the specific "crime" which is involved is indicated in the epic by the "noise" (*rigmu*) and the "tumult" (*ḫubūru*) made by humans (I. 358–359), accompaniments, as Oden sees it, of rebellion against a divinely established order which imposed on humans at creation the status of laborers for the gods.[9] But the rebellion is doomed to failure and the outcome of the Flood, and the conclusion of the epic, is the establishment of regulations which will prevent a recurrence of the rebellion and finally demarcate the two realms. Such is Oden's overall interpretation of the epic; and, while we cannot accept it, especially the notion that human rebellion is the pretext for Enlil's decision to destroy humanity,[10] the important point is that Oden sees the same theme at work in the PH, which consists in "a collection of several instances of the human propensity to trespass

7. Among them, Clark, "The Flood," 184–88 and B. F. Batto's contribution to this volume. See also the bibliography cited by Oden, "Divine Aspirations," 204–208. Others for whom the issue in Atrahasis is overpopulation and the cosmic imbalance which this entails include R. S. Hendel, "Of Demigods and the Deluge: Toward an Interpretation of Genesis 6:1–4," *JBL* 106 (1987) 17, 23–25, and H. N. Wallace, *The Eden Narrative* (HSM 32; Atlanta: Scholars, 1985) 34. On Westermann, see below, n. 18.

8. Oden, "Divine Aspirations," 200, 208.

9. Ibid., 210.

10. This is not the place to rehearse all the arguments against Oden's interpretation here. See, however, most recently, W. L. Moran, "Some Considerations of Form and Interpretation in Atra-Ḥasīs," *Language, Literature, and History: Philological and Historical Studies Presented to Erica Reiner* (AOS 67; ed. F. Rochberg-Halton; New Haven: AOS, 1987) 251–55. In addition to Moran's comments, one might ask if measures taken to reduce humankind's numbers are any way to deal with the issue at hand, i.e., its tendency to overreach.

upon the divine sphere."[11] The key biblical texts are Gen 11:1–9; 2:4b–3:24; and 6:1–4.

A. Gen 11:1–9

As Oden sees it, the human aspiration for divine status is transparent in 11:1–9, where the top of the tower "assaults the sky—a perfect and natural metaphor for the human assault upon the divinely ordained cosmos."[12] Wallace concurs: for him, too, "the important aspect about the tower . . . is that it has its head in heaven . . . an intrusion by humankind into the realm of divine beings otherwise not his domain." And so, Yahweh steps in to remove the intrusion and to prevent further ones by placing limitations on humankind, namely, its dispersion through the earth and the multiplication of its languages.[13]

As we see it, there can be no doubt in the story about Yahweh's displeasure at what the humans are doing; indeed, Yahweh exclaims, "This is only their beginning . . . !" (11:6).[14] But it is not at all obvious that what they intend to do is to force their way into heaven. After all, the text explicitly describes the humans as engaged only in building a "city with a tower" (hendiadys),[15] vv 4 and 5, or only a "city" (v 8). Not once is there talk merely of constructing a tower. In other words, at issue is the building of a mighty city, a truly "monumental architectural work," whose magnitude is expressed with customary hyperbole by stressing its tower's height (cf. Deut 1:28).[16] And the avowed motive of the humans is equally mundane, namely, the "fame" that comes through doing outstanding deeds (cf. 2 Sam 8:13) (v 4). Such fame as comes with the building of an impressive city might, of course, be treated positively in Mesopotamian texts (viz., the beginning and end of Gilgamesh), but within the Bible such works, in particular, come to be seen as the very embodiment

11. Oden, "Divine Aspirations," 211.

12. Ibid.

13. Wallace, "The Eden Narrative" (Ph.D. diss., Harvard, 1982) 229–30.

14. It seems important to emphasize, against Westermann (*Genesis: A Commentary* [3 vols.; Minneapolis: Augsburg, 1984] 1. 551), that the building of the city cannot be excluded from the purpose of God's intervention, as if that intervention were directed only at what people may do in the future, a kind of preventive "first-strike."

15. Ibid., 547, following E. A. Speiser.

16. G. von Rad, *Genesis* (OTL; Philadelphia: Westminster, 1972) 147; Westermann, *Genesis*, 547–48.

of sinful pride (Isa 2:12–15; 13:19; 23:8–14; Jer 51:53; Amos 6:8). That is surely the provocation here for God's intervention: a pride of the kind Israel's wisdom tradition and the Psalms, in particular, repeatedly associate with the conduct of the wicked (Prov 8:13; Ps 73:6) who hotly pursue the afflicted without fear (Ps 10:2–6) and whose outrages know no bounds (Ps 73:3–12). Thus, there is no fear here on God's part of "intrusion" into his realm or of a mixing of the divine and the human;[17] rather, there is a refusal by God to endorse the project of the great city, from time immemorial an emblem of human culture and civilization, a refusal to endorse the significance of what *has* been achieved within it. As such, it is a refusal which can look explicitly to the future ("nothing that they presume to do will be impossible for them," v 6), reflectively, out of a disillusionment with the past. To borrow a phrase from von Rad,[18] this is really a bit of "cultural history" by the Yahwist, an assertion of the role that a sinful pride has played in motivating the great works of civilization, in the end to the detriment of humankind rather than to its glory.

B. Gen 2:4b–3:24

If humans' divine aspirations are not as "transparent" in Genesis 2–3, the narrative in many respects appears to give more credence to the theme of the "mixing of the divine and human worlds," such that "whenever there is the possibility of a mixing of the divine and human worlds, Yahweh is portrayed as the *antagonist* [italics mine] of humankind, stepping in and placing further limitations on the latter."[19] Here, Clark, for example, finds in 3:22, 24, in conjunction with the Tree of Life, one of only two occurrences in the PH of the motif of "divine protection against potential

17. Clark ("The Flood," 192) regards "the reconstruction of a functional myth behind Gen 11:1–9 in which the revolt against the gods plays a meaningful role" as dubious. Westermann (*Genesis,* 1. 53, 554–55), too, regards the "encroachment" theme in this sense as secondary to the idea that the great city represents human ambition. However, Westermann seems to want to have it both ways when he asserts that, although this human ambition is *not* itself reprehensible or directed against God, Gen 11:1–9 (like Genesis 2–3) shows that humans when left to themselves are in grave danger (because of their "aspiration to burst their created limits"): this aspiration merely "hides within itself the possibility of overstepping the limits." One must ask too how, for Westermann, this incident represents "the arrogant abuse of technology" (p. 53).

18. von Rad, *Genesis,* 151.

19. Wallace, "The Eden Narrative" (Ph.D. diss.), 235–36.

or actual human revolt which threatens the position of the gods,"[20] whereas Oden sees in the Knowledge of Good and Evil (Gen 2:9, 17; 3:5, 22), interpreted as a "knowledge of all things" (*merismus*), Adam and Eve's aspiration for divine status.[21] Apparently, the knowledge in question amounts to a kind of omniscience, something clearly beyond the reach of mortals. As such, it, along with the immortality of the Tree of Life (2:9), demarcates the boundary between the human and the divine realms, whose violation produces the world as we know it.

What is not at issue in this study is the clear etiological thrust of the narrative and the way in which this reveals the difference between human-kind and the gods. Comparison with the gods is, after all, explicit in the case of knowledge (3:5) and, at least, implicit in the case of life (3:22). The question is how hard and fast the boundaries are here, and, even more so, to what extent the concern of the narrative really is to draw them. As Adapa or Gilgamesh suggest, the linkage of the motifs of knowledge and life are far from accidental; and, in the ancient Near East, the former was often associated with opportunities lost by humankind for gaining immortality. Knowledge acquired and life lost: it is an age-old theme in ancient Near Eastern literature:

> To him [Adapa] he [Ea] had given wisdom;
> eternal life he had not given him.[22]

The Genesis narrative, in other words, stands in a tradition in which human existence is defined in relation to these two possibilities, two ways in which conceivably humans might be like the gods.[23] To be sure, there was no ambiguity in the tradition about which of those two possibilities was viable; life was in the hands of the gods. But it was humankind's divine-like knowledge that also separated mortals from the animal world:

> Thou art [wi]se, Enkidu, art become like a god! Why with the wild creatures dost thou roam over the steppe? (I iv 34–35)[24]

20. Clark, "The Flood," 191.
21. Oden, "Divine Aspirations," 211–13; so also Wallace (*Eden Narrative,* 115–24), who, like Oden, does not wish to restrict it to cultural knowledge.
22. *ANET,* 101.
23. So too Westermann, *Genesis,* 272.
24. *ANET,* 75.

This much the narrative presumes. But whereas in the Mesopotamian epic tradition wisdom functions as a kind of "consolation" for the loss of immortal life (viz., Adapa, Gilgamesh), in Eden the acquisition of this same knowledge provokes its loss.[25] In other words, the narrative simply assumes the differences and the relations only to explore them in an entirely unconventional way. Despite the serpent's effort to inject a note of rivalry into the relationship of God to his creatures ("You will not die! But God knows when you eat of it . . . you will be like gods knowing good and evil" [3:4b–5]), the motive for the expulsion from the garden, God's own dwelling,[26] is not God's "antagonism" to humankind — but Adam and Eve's disobedience of God's unambiguous command (2:17; cf. 3:17). For the narrative, the obvious limitations of human existence (pain, toil, and death) are, ironically, traceable to human guilt.

This becomes clearer when we recognize that human aspirations for a divine status are not nearly so obvious in the text as commentators are wont to suggest. Aside from the fact that Eve's motives do not explicitly resume the serpent's remarks about knowledge's godlike character (3:6), the identification of the knowledge involved as a kind of omniscience is highly questionable. With Westermann, it must be said that the man and the woman represent humankind in its origin and, therefore, in its present condition. As such, there is no basis in the text for an elevation of 'ādām's condition over historical humanity.[27] Key, to our mind, is the acknowledgment by Yahweh in 3:22 that 'ādām has indeed "become like one of us," a comment which is not congruent with the view that the knowledge in question is omniscience and that "to become like gods in any way far surpasses the attainment of human maturity in any form."[28]

If so, what, then, is "the knowledge of good and evil"? As Wellhausen remarked long ago, the expression designates, first and foremost, the knowledge simply of what is helpful or hurtful for humankind.[29] In other words, this is an achievement which is in some real sense analogous to the attainment of adult experience and adult responsibility (cf. Deut 1:39;

25. Damrosch, *Narrative Covenant,* 132.

26. Wallace, *Eden Narrative,* 70–88.

27. Westermann, *Genesis,* 241.

28. Wallace, *Eden Narrative,* 117.

29. J. Wellhausen, *Prolegomena to the History of Ancient Israel* (tr. Black and Menzies; Gloucester: Peter Smith, 1973) 302. On the syntax of the full name of the tree, *ʿēs haddaʿat ṭôb wārāʿ,* see Wallace, *Eden Narrative,* 115–16.

Isa 7:15).[30] As such, "to become like God" does not represent a condition over and above knowledge, but describes knowledge itself in its general and comprehensive sense,[31] or, as some have put it, "cultural" knowledge.[32] Adam and Eve simply choose to have the knowledge that is proper to humankind, that knowledge which likens them to the gods and sets them apart from all else on earth. Their aspiration is not for a change of ontological status; and so their transgression cannot be understood as hubris.[33]

To be sure, the knowledge Adam and Eve obtain in disobedience does mark a higher stage of *human* development; but it is "progress" in the Yahwistic critique of culture which comes only at a terrible price, namely, "the loss of simple obedience" (von Rad).[34] Wellhausen noted the same long ago:

> As the human race goes forward in civilisation, it goes backward in the fear of God. The first step in civilisation is clothing; and here this is the first result of the fall.[35]

Adam and Eve had life in the garden; but in choosing knowledge over straightforward obedience, they choose a world in which such human achievement stands under a shadow. Humankind is expelled in 3:23 from the garden and so from proximity to God. But in 3:22, 24 another motive for the expulsion has been added to the original conclusion in 3:23,[36] namely, the prevention of Adam from eating of the Tree of Life and so living forever. Prior to this the Tree of Life had not been subject to any prohibition by God (cf. 2:17), perhaps ironically so. The author's irony concerning the wisdom of human choice could not be more telling. When

---

30. I. Höver-Johag, "*ṭôb*," *TDOT* 5. 309. Wallace (*Eden Narrative,* 127–28) lays great stress on 2 Sam 19:36 as critical for the interpretation of the phrase here under discussion. However, not only is his rendering of Barzillai's response doubtful ("he no longer knows anything"), but he fails to comment on the difference in the grammatical constructions (*ha'ēda' bên-ṭôb lĕrā'*).

31. Westermann, *Genesis,* 240.

32. Thus von Rad, *Genesis,* 101; Wellhausen, *Prolegomena,* 302.

33. If human knowledge here represents an "encroachment" upon the divine, it is puzzling that God leaves the human pair with the "fruit" of their theft.

34. von Rad, *Genesis,* 101.

35. Wellhausen, *Prolegomena,* 302.

36. For this analysis, see Westermann, *Genesis,* 271–73.

faced with an unambiguous choice between life and death, humankind—in the name of wisdom—chooses death![37]

Why should the Tree of Life now become unavailable? Clark sees here, though not originally,[38] the "motif of divine protection against potential or actual human revolt which threatens the position of the gods." Wallace goes so far as to contend that the expulsion is not so much concerned with Adam and Eve's disobedience as it is the new state of humankind (viz., 3:22, "the man has become like one of us") and the potential for "further change undesirable from God's perspective."[39] As a motive, all of this seems to bear out what the serpent had suggested to Eve in 3:5. And to the same degree it is also suspect. Though the motif was evidently available to the Yahwist from 3:5, he is "strangely" reticent about introducing it in 3:22, 24 with any explicitness. Thereby, the unavailability of the Tree of Life (which the narrative's etiological intention asserts is the present difference between gods and humankind) looks less like the attempt to demarcate two realms, or even God's anxiety about his position, than—in view of 2:17—precisely a punishment for humankind's disobedience, one which is effected through alienation from God's presence. But, as Westermann remarks, this need not mean a definitive separation.[40] And the priestly comment on the fate of Enoch in Gen 5:24 (itself perhaps old tradition) would seem to suggest the same.

C. Gen 6:1–4

Gen 6:1–4 is the third narrative to be considered, whose story, it has been said, "could hardly articulate more transparently . . . the theme of the forbidden nature of divine human mixing,"[41] and "imbalance and a

37. Note the frequent juxtaposition of wisdom and life in the wisdom teaching of the two ways (viz., Prov 2:5–22; 4:10–18). Here their normal relationship is entirely reversed to teach a wisdom which lies in obedience (Prov 1:7; 9:10).

38. Clark ("The Flood," 191–92) thinks Genesis 3 originally did not contain the revolt motif, but it was extended to Genesis 3 from the Mesopotamian flood tradition.

39. Wallace, "The Eden Narrative" (Ph.D. diss.), 228.

40. Westermann, *Genesis,* 277.

41. Oden, "Divine Aspirations," 214. But in apparent acknowledgment of the fact that the incident is provoked by the "sons of God," Oden contends that their offspring "bear the same genetic mix as the first humans in Atrahasis and therefore the same propensity to rebellion." This view is not shared by others who see here the problem of divine-human mixing: Clark ("The Flood," 192), for whom the point is "the illustration of the theme

confusion in the cosmic order."[42] Regardless of whether the story is to be understood as supplying the immediate motivation for the Flood, as some believe,[43] or simply, as we take it, another example of the "evil imagination" of humanity,[44] the question is whether in the story Yahweh is reacting to the "contact" between the divine and the human realm or to something else. In view of the text's laconic nature and a preliterary history which is far from clear, one cannot be certain. But as Hendel has recently noted, the text certainly contains no overt references to the separation of gods and mortals[45] and nothing to suggest specifically "divine aspirations" on the part of humans, who here are the victims of rape by divine beings ("they took for themselves wives from whomever they chose," 2b). That Yahweh is displeased with what comes from the union of these promiscuous beings and human women is clear, not only from the notice of the rape (v 2b above), but from the limitation of human life span in v 3. And just as certainly, Yahweh acts here to limit the strength/potential of humanity, including those *gibbōrîm* born of the union (whose origin seems to have been the point of the original story contained in vv 1–2, 4b).[46] But that Yahweh does this out of a desire to keep the divine and the human realms apart is by no means a necessary explanation. Indeed, if that were his goal, action against the instigators of the crime, namely the "sons of God," would be more appropriate. Instead, the focus in 6:1–4 is on humankind, because the cause for concern is there, where these demigods have now been let loose on earth.

To be sure, such beings can be regarded as beneficent, as in classical sources (viz., Heracles, Theseus) apparently they are, or even in Mesopotamia (Gilgamesh). But in the Bible they appear in a more ambiguous light. Ezekiel 32:27, where the Nephilim and "the warriors" may be identified as they seem to be in Gen 6:1–4, is instructive (cf. Num 13:33): "for

of no contact with the divine"; Hendel, "Of Demigods," 23; von Rad, *Genesis*, 115; Wallace, "The Eden Narrative" (Ph.D. diss.) 224–35; Westermann (*Genesis*, 369), who sees in v 3 the violation of "limits."

42. Hendel, "Of Demigods," 23.

43. Clark, "The Flood," 192; Oden, "Divine Aspirations," 214; von Rad, *Genesis*, 116–17.

44. Hendel ("Of Demigods," 23–24), who thinks that J had detached 6:1–4 from the flood story where it originally served as its motivation; Wallace, "The Eden Narrative" (Ph.D. diss.) 233–36; Westermann, *Genesis*, 368.

45. Hendel, "Of Demigods," 21.

46. On the literary structure of the text, see, for example, Westermann, *Genesis*, 365–68.

(the) terror of (the) warriors (*gibbōrîm*) was on the land of (the) living."[47] In 1 Enoch 7:3–6, too, in the course of a theologically oriented exposition of Gen 6:1–4,[48] the giants who are produced by the union of the heavenly beings and humans quickly turn on the inhabitants of the earth, which they proceed to fill with bloodshed and oppression until the earth cries out to heaven against them (9:1). In other words, in Gen 6:1–4, the object of God's limitation on humanity's vitality seems to be an already violence-prone humanity now "supercharged," as it were, by semi-divine beings. As such, Gen 6:1–4 offers but one more instance of the degeneration of creation and human culture which has been portrayed in the PH's unnerving story of humankind's adventure in civilization.

To summarize our argument thus far: a close examination of Gen 2:4b–3:24; 6:1–4; and 11:1–9 does not show the violation of ontologically defined boundaries to be a single and consistent theme of the Yahwist's PH nor does it show his effort to be directed to the divinely ordained separation of heaven and earth as two distinct realms. That is not the ancient world and we should not expect it to be the Yahwist's. To be sure, there are tensions and oppositions between God and humanity in these stories, but the interpreter's articulation of these oppositions cannot be turned into metaphysics, theological or literary. For the oppositions are subordinate to the Yahwist's illustration of something else, not highlighted when "border crossing" and "encroachment" becomes the message of J. Adam and Eve *disobey* God (cf. 3:17), not "encroach" upon divine territory. Cain *kills* Abel (4:8), not simply "oversteps" the proper bounds between brothers.[49] Such language is emotionally charged and evaluative, underscoring, as we have already suggested, the Yahwist's engagement in an effort, not simply to recount but to weigh the progress of humankind and to characterize it. J juxtaposes God and humankind, and there is definition by means of the comparison. But "two realms" are not simply juxtaposed. Humanity's past cultural achievement is evaluated, evaluated in ways which reverse to a great extent the kind of endorsement given in Mesopotamian epic texts, among them Atrahasis.

---

47. On the text and the possibility of reading *nĕpīlîm* for MT *nōpĕlîm,* see W. Zimmerli, *Ezekiel* (2 vols.; Hermeneia; Philadelphia: Fortress, 1983) 2. 168.

48. On 1 Enoch 6–11's relation to the Genesis text, see Hanson, "Rebellion in Heaven," esp. 196–202.

49. Cf. Hendel, "Of Demigods," 24–25.

III. Westermann and the Yahwist's "Desacralization of Culture"

Although Westermann is wont to speak of "limits" and "revolt" in connection with the stories of the PH, indeed to view the latter as a "series of stories of crime and punishment to illustrate the various ways in which a creature can revolt against the creator,"[50] for the most part, neither he, nor his former student R. Albertz, are to be grouped with those whose position we have examined above. For Westermann, the "limits" are conceived theologically as established with humanity's creation, while the "revolt" in question is generally not regarded as a *literal* "encroachment" of an ontologically established divine realm but as the human aspiration to "burst" its created limits and seek autonomy from God.[51] Nonetheless, in one aspect, Westermann's understanding of the PH does involve him in an effort to separate the divine and the human in a way which is of thematic importance for understanding Genesis 2–11. It becomes apparent when Westermann insists on the Yahwist's "desacralization" of all cultural achievement: "Faced with the mythology of the Ancient Near East, the Bible takes the same stand as does the modern secular historian; all progress in civilization is a human achievement."[52]

While one winces at the idea of the Yahwist as a "modern secular historian," Westermann has hit upon an important point. J's stories depicting the progress of civilization make no mention at all of a divine origin of the arts of cattle breeding, horticulture, or metallurgy (Gen 4:17–26) even as Mesopotamian myths praise the gods because they are the creators of the pick-axe and the plough. Where in Atrahasis the specialized skills necessary for irrigation agriculture (I.21f., 338) are developed by the gods and later transferred to humans who have been expressly created to relieve lower-ranking gods of the toil the gods' sustenance requires (I.196, 339; cf. III.iii.30–31), in the Yahwist's PH, God is in no way dependent upon human labor, which is entirely "profane," i.e., intended to serve only human interests.[53] Humans do not learn the arts of civilization from

50. Westermann, *Genesis,* 53.

51. See, for example, Westermann's treatment of this specific point in connection with Genesis 2–3 (ibid., 248) or the Tower of Babel (ibid., 548–49, 554–55).

52. Ibid., 61.

53. R. Albertz, "Die Kulturarbeit im Atramḫasīs im Vergleich zur biblischen Urgeschichte," *Werden und Wirken des Alten Testaments* (ed. R. Albertz, H-P. Müller, H. W. Wolff, and W. Zimmerli; Göttingen: Vandenhoeck & Ruprecht, 1900) 46–47.

seven antediluvian sages (*apkallū*);[54] though traceable back to a divine commission (cf. Gen 2:8, 15), human discoveries and inventions remain thoroughly human and lack any sacral character.[55]

This "secularization" of human work and art in the Bible is, of course, of profound theological significance for both Albertz and Westermann,[56] and in no way suggests a negative attitude on the part of the Bible to cultural achievement. Quite the contrary! But in view of the unambiguous endorsement of such achievement by the gods in Mesopotamian epic, Westermann also seems somewhat embarrassed by the lack of any straightforward approval in J. He can only point to the fact that, despite disobedience and punishment, humanity is still left with life and its vital power; or, in the context of 4:17–26, which presents a history of humankind's cultural achievements framed by the murder of Abel and the braggart song of Lamech, he can only cite Deut 6:10 ("great and good cities which you did not build").[57] This cannot be right.

Westermann is, of course, aware of the pall that the Song of Lamech (4:23–24), for example, casts upon the genealogy of civilization in 4:17–26. But his statement that this constitutes merely an expression of the negative possibilities inherent in cultural progress does not go far enough.[58] In the context of the optimistic and affirmative attitudes of Mesopotamian epic toward cultural achievement,[59] the decidedly negative frame the Yahwist puts up around the genealogy of culture heroes in 4:17–24, brings about a reversal of the values associated with humankind's cultural history, a refusal to assess that history positively.[60]

In addition, while much attention has been focused in recent years on the structural and thematic similarities of Atrahasis and the PH, not enough attention has been paid, in our opinion, to the overall theological conception of Atrahasis and to how its viewpoint is completely missing

---

54. E. Reiner, "The Etiological Myth of the 'Seven Sages,'" *Or* 30 (1961) 1–11; W. G. Lambert, "Ancestors, Authors, and Canonicity," *JCS* 11 (1957) 8–9.

55. Albertz, "Die Kulturarbeit," 45; Westermann, *Genesis,* 61, 342–44.

56. Westermann, *Genesis,* 67.

57. Ibid., 61, 327–28.

58. Ibid., 336–37, 343–44.

59. T. Jacobsen, "The Eridu Genesis," *JBL* 100 (1981) 526–29.

60. Is it significant that only the initiation of the Yahwistic cult, with the birth of Enosh to Seth in vv 25–26, stands outside the frame formed by the murder of Abel and the Song of Lamech?

in the Genesis narrative. Indeed, the disparagement of the gods' behavior in Atrahasis is the antithesis of the biblical portrayal of the deity and ought to be seen as integral to the epic's reflection on humankind's place in the universe. If in Atrahasis the gods come to recognize their folly in sending the Flood (III.iii.36–43, v. 36–43), in the Bible God regrets the creation of humankind (Gen 6:6).

Thus, in marked contrast to Yahweh's acceptance of a flawed humanity in the post-flood world (8:21–22) is the gods' acceptance in Atrahasis of their *need* of humankind, a need they should have realized before the onset of stomach cramps (III.iii.28–31).[61] Without the offerings of the humans they have thoughtlessly destroyed (III.v.42–43), the gods are wasted by hunger and feverish with thirst, to the point that they swarm over the offering of Atrahasis like flies (III.v.34–35). And so, while in the Genesis narrative it is the depravity of humankind which comes in for censure (6:5; 8:21), at the conclusion of Atrahasis it is the unthinking and foolish decision of Enlil, executive of the gods. It is Enlil's decision to bring on the flood that is castigated as evil (*lemnu*), and it is his utterance that is deplored as abominable (*bīšu*) (III.iii.39–40). By portraying the folly of the gods as the backdrop for the Deluge, the epic affirms humankind and its essential place in the cosmic scheme.

In the Bible, however, God has no "need" of humanity, and the only censure is reserved for humankind. Indeed, as Damrosch, among others, rightly observes, the Yahwist's work in Genesis 2–11 assumes almost an "anti-epic" quality in its assertion of the questionableness of cultural achievement and human progress.[62]

This begins with Genesis 2–3. In contrast to the thoroughly positive treatment the acquisition of knowledge receives in Gilgamesh's depiction of primitive human beginnings, in the famous scene of Enkidu's seduction by the harlot (I iv),[63] Adam and Eve come to shame upon eating the fruit of the Tree of Knowledge (see above), and the clothes they wear—for Enkidu, an emblem of civilized life—become the mark of their disgrace. Thereupon, a murder takes place amid the rivalry accompanying

61. W. L. Moran, "Atrahasis: The Babylonian Story of the Flood," *Bib* 52 (1971) 59.

62. Damrosch, *Narrative Covenant*, 134; cf. van Seters, *In Search of History: Historiography in the Ancient World and the Origins of Biblical History* (New Haven: Yale, 1983) 25–31. I am indebted to Damrosch at a number of points in the following discussion.

63. *ANET*, 75.

the diversification of human labor into farming and animal husbandry (4:1–16). And then, in the genealogy of civilization which follows (vv 17–26), it turns out to be the murderer Cain (or his son Enoch?) who is explicitly credited with founding the first city (4:17).[64] In this context, is it a cause for wonder that the offspring of Lamech turn out to be the ancestors of musicians and all who forge metal instruments (4:19–22)? Or that the cultivation of the vine, which was intended to bring relief from human work (5:29), leads instead to the degradation of the cultivator by his own son (9:20–27)? In Gilgamesh (Atrahasis?) Utnapishtim takes care to board all manner of craftsmen onto the ark (XI.ii.85),[65] but no such provision is made for their survival in the Bible. How can this be a story of the emancipation of human endeavor from myth as Westermann claims?

In sum, the persistent contrast the Bible presents to the epic tradition is an unabashedly negative assessment of human civilization and cultural progress. Where the city of Babylon functions in Enuma Elish as the symbol *par excellence* of the gods' validation of human culture, built by the gods themselves (VI 50–90),[66] in Genesis 11:1–9 it is parodied as a place of confusion (v 9) humans built, in a vain effort to win glory and to protect themselves "lest we be scattered all over the earth" (v 4).[67]

For Westermann and Albertz, the theme of culture constitutes only a marginal theme in the Yahwist's PH, one which in contrast to Mesopotamia would have all but disappeared were it not for Gen 11:1–9 and brief genealogical addenda (4:2, 17b, 20b, 21, 22; 9:20; 10:8, 9).[68] It remains subordinate to the Yahwist's intention to portray "the various ways in which the creature can revolt against the creator," individually or as a community, through a "series" of crime and punishment stories.[69] This is not the place to offer a thorough critique of Westermann's understanding of the Yahwist's intent.[70] Let it simply be noted that it abstracts

64. One expects the founder to be Cain's son. On the problem, see Westermann, *Genesis*, 327.

65. *ANET*, 94.

66. Ibid., 68.

67. Damrosch, *Narrative Covenant*, 134.

68. Westermann, *Genesis*, 11; Albertz, "Die Kulturarbeit," 45–46.

69. Westermann, *Genesis*, 53.

70. For such a critique, particularly of the scheme of sin and punishment, see Clark, "The Flood," 188–97; Wallace, "The Eden Narrative" (Ph.D. diss.) 227–31.

from what is decisive structurally in the PH, namely the conjunction of genealogy and narrative to produce not just a "collection," or "series," of exemplary stories which show the various ways in which humans rebel against God,[71] but a historiographically oriented narrative about human beginnings from the creation of a primal couple to the spread of humankind through the earth. The Yahwist's genealogies have the effect, beyond relating peoples and tribes to each other, of ordering his narratives into a loose chronology which connects the distant past of human beginnings to the more recent historic times of a world the Yahwist knows.[72]

But again the goal is not simply to report: it is to assess. Indeed, one might say that "history" becomes here the vehicle of assessment, an assessment of humankind's past historical experience in which, contrary to Westermann, the theme of culture and the progress of civilization figure prominently.[73] The problem for Westermann and Albertz is that here human knowledge, the civilized arts, and the achievements of culture fall under a judgment which becomes theologically problematic, since they wish to stress that civilization and its effects have in themselves a positive emphasis in Israel from the beginning.[74] Thus, the talk of "secularization." But the Yahwist does not share their concern for the relation of science to theology or anything like it: rather, his concern is to critique in the strongest terms possible humankind's past and its accomplishments, a "past" which is also Israel's "past" and prologue to her history, and equally a mirror to her present.

Regardless of whether Damrosch is correct to speak of Genesis 2–11 as a "creation-flood epic," he is surely right in seeing that by reworking old "creation-flood epics" like Atrahasis and Gilgamesh, J creates a kind of anti-epic that questions the achievements of the peoples of the past and that opens the way to the probing of earthly institutions which is central to Hebrew historiography.[75] And it is this questioning of the past

71. Westermann, *Genesis,* 53–54.

72. On the function of genealogy in ancient historiography and in the early narrative strands of Genesis 1–11 specifically, see J. van Seters, *In Search of History,* 11–31.

73. This kind of assessment, of course, is proper to history writing. Again, see here van Seters, *In Search of History,* 1–6.

74. Westermann, *Genesis,* 342–43; Albertz, "Die Kulturarbeit," 55–57.

75. Damrosch, *Narrative Covenant,* 134–35. I cannot, however, agree with Damrosch (137–42) when he seeks to show that Genesis 2–11 develops the theme that human culture

that more than anything else runs through the PH, which often enough lacks precisely those features of sin and punishment Westermann's understanding of the Yahwist's intent requires (note in this regard only Gen 6:1–4 and Gen 11:1–9).

IV. Conclusion

To conclude that the Yahwist is not intent upon depicting the divinely ordained separation of heaven and earth as two distinct realms is, as suggested at the outset, of no little importance to a theological anthropology which seeks to be biblically grounded. But equally noteworthy is the understanding achieved by comparing the Yahwist's work in the PH with epic texts from Mesopotamia. Although such a comparison does not offer to the biblical theologian eager for the *rapprochement* of Christian theology and contemporary culture, including its technology, the possibility of easy generalizations about the Bible's attitude, this difficulty is a sign of the maturity that now characterizes comparative study of the Bible. Polemical interests have too often in the past distorted both the interpretation of the Bible and the world from which it emerged.

In any case, it must be remembered that the Yahwist's effort to articulate the beginnings of our world and human cultural life do not arise in a vacuum, and this is something any theology of creation must be alert to. While the authors of the Bible's creation stories could be said to possess a speculative interest, that interest never achieved the status of science and remained subordinate to a concern for understanding the present, if not immediate, moment and its context. As a result, creation accounts in the Bible and the ancient Near East functioned as topics, or themes, dependent upon some other context; and they were always tailored to serve some other purpose than to generalize about creation itself, e.g., to glorify a god, to explain a phenomenon, to legitimize a value or a practice.[76] They might even be used, as in case of the Yahwist's PH, to criticize an age or to serve as the foil to another.

---

is a product merely of the "existential state" of separation from God, a process of separation which begins with Adam's creation and, in fact, leads to his guilt. The characters of PH are not, as Damrosch concludes, emblems of merely "existential" problems in the relation of humanity to God. J is explicit about what the problem in the relationship is: the problem is human evil (Gen 6:5).

76. Clifford, "Creation in the Hebrew Bible," 151–52.

RICHARD J. CLIFFORD, S.J.

Creation in
the Psalms

The theological meaning of creation in the psalms has only recently attracted the interest of many scholars.[1] Paradoxically, seeds of the lively contemporary interest were sown by Gerhard von Rad's 1936 essay that sought to minimize the significance of creation in Psalms and Second Isaiah. For von Rad creation was a late import into the Bible, gaining significance only from its relation to the concept of redemption; only in Psalms 19 and 104 was creation an independent concept.[2] Von Rad raised the question in an interesting way: did creation have any real (i.e., redemptive) significance or did it provide merely illustrative contrast? Several factors since then have moved creation to center stage. Scholarly interest in creation in Second Isaiah, which von Rad himself helped stir up, led naturally to the Psalter as one source of the prophet's literary forms and ideas.[3] Meanwhile new respect for biblical wisdom literature beginning in the 1960's provided scholars with a new theological category, "creation," to complement the previously dominant banner of "history."

1. In his 1974 survey of research Rainer Albertz noted how little had been done, apart from the "Catholic works" of G. Lambert, E. Beaucamp, L. Legrand, and B. Rigaux, in his *Weltschöpfung und Menschenschöpfung: Untersucht bei Deuterojesaja, Hiob und in den Psalmen* (Calwer Theologische Monographien 3; Stuttgart: Calwer, 1974) 176 n. 1. Since then have appeared H.-J. Kraus, *Theology of the Psalms* (Augsburg: Minneapolis, 1986) 59–67 and T. E. Fretheim, "Nature's Praise of God in the Psalms," *Ex Auditu* 3 (1988) 16–30.

2. In *The Problem of the Hexateuch and Other Essays* (New York: McGraw-Hill, 1966).

3. This is the approach of Albertz, *Weltschöpfung*.

Proverbs, Job, Qoheleth, and Sirach could be studied theologically because they had to do with creation.[4]

This essay continues the investigation of creation, narrowing the focus to the Psalter, and more specifically to two genres of the Psalter—the communal lament and the hymn. The focus on genre is deliberate. As even a cursory look at ancient Near Eastern literature shows, creation accounts or cosmogonies[5] are determined by the genre they are found in. A cosmogony in an incantation, for example, performs differently from a cosmogony in an astrological text or in an epic. The psalms of the Bible, convention-bound and stereotyped like most liturgical literature, must be read with awareness of their genre. Singling out two of the many genres in the Psalter also has the advantage of limiting a potentially diffuse topic.

The topic and the focus of this essay coincide to a remarkable degree with the 1974 monograph of Rainer Albertz, *Weltschöpfung und Menschenschöpfung: Untersucht bei Deutero-jesaja, Hiob und in den Psalmen,* a slight revision of a doctoral dissertation done under the direction of Claus Westermann. Albertz concluded that for Psalms as for Second Isaiah there were two distinct creation traditions—creation of the world (*Weltschöpfung*) and creation of the individual human being (*Menschenschöpfung*). The former tradition is found in the genre of hymn where it serves to emphasize Yahweh's majesty. The latter occurs in the genre of lament where it is the basis for appeals to Yahweh's mercy, something like "Do not abandon the person you have created." Not until in the postexilic period did the two traditions come together and then only rarely, e.g., Neh 9:6 and Zech 12:1. Albertz's sharp distinction between the two creation traditions is derived from his analysis of Second Isaiah and of Sumero-Babylonian, Egyptian, and primitive prayers.[6]

This essay comes to conclusions quite different from Albertz's. His distinction between two creation traditions is not substantiated in the comparative literatures[7] and is not valid for the communal lament and

---

4. G. von Rad, *Wisdom in Israel* (Nashville: Abingdon, 1972).

5. The concern of this essay is with cosmogonies, accounts of the coming into existence of the world, not with every reference to creation.

6. Albertz, *Weltschöpfung.* He owes the distinction to his teacher C. Westermann, who develops it in his *Isaiah 40–66* (OTL; Philadelphia: Westminster, 1969) 24–26 and in *Genesis 1–11: A Commentary* (Minneapolis: Augsburg, 1984) 19–25.

7. I will offer a detailed criticism of the Westermann-Albertz distinction in a forthcoming book in the Biblica et Orientalia series. The most serious general objection is that many

the hymn. My differences from Albertz on how cosmogonies function in the two genres will become evident in the analyses of individual psalms below. Before dealing with specific psalms, however, his general distinction between creation of the world and of human beings must be examined.

The preliminary question is how creation is to be defined. The first step toward a definition is to notice relevant differences between ancient and modern conception. Modern operating definitions are imbued with evolutionary and scientific assumptions. These assumptions must be assessed in order to understand what ancient composers meant by their creation accounts. Most of the important differences have already been detailed in the introductory essay so only a few points need to be mentioned here.

Ancient Near Eastern cosmogonies are concerned with the origin of the world of ordinary experience—the here and now world of the gods and of human society. They speak of how the two realms relate to each another. The perspective of most texts is theocentric or (ultimately the same viewpoint) templocentric. Human beings were created to serve the gods, which meant building and maintaining their palaces (frequently under the direction of the king). The perspective at the same time is often ethnocentric; the society in question is not the human race as such but a particular people or nation, e.g., Babylon, Israel.

The activity of the gods was generally imagined on the model of human activity or of natural processes. The gods acted like human beings, exhibiting basically the same loves, hates, passions, and ambitions that drive human beings. The account of creation could thus be a story with the same dramatic movement as stories about human beings. It was not objective description. The criterion of truth of the narratives was dramatic plausibility rather than scientific accuracy. Many different and even contradictory versions of creation were reverently copied and preserved.

These remarks about modern and ancient Near Eastern conceptions bear directly on cosmogonies in the Psalter. Since the ancient evidence shows that cosmogonies can be stories about the gods making the world of temples and human beings for their use and comfort, one expects the psalm cosmogonies to be not only about the physical universe but a

ancient cosmogonies were systems that included anthropogonies. Separate anthropogonies existed, of course, but that fact does not warrant a universal distinction of two traditions. Albertz, it is true, refers to creation generally, whereas this essay refers to cosmogonies only but the critique of the distinction is nonetheless valid.

peopled universe. And the human community is imagined concretely, structured with kingship, land, language, god, and laws.[8] It is well known that many psalms contain historical accounts of Israel's origins, pre-eminently the exodus from Egypt and taking of Canaan (sometimes only by allusion), e.g., Pss 44:2–9; 66:5–9; 74:1–2; 77:16; 78:42–54; 80:9–12; 105; 135; 136; 149. It is not always noticed that several of the little histories in these psalms mix historical and cosmogonic language, e.g., Pss 77:17–21 and 89:6–38. Some psalms use predominantly cosmogonic language, e.g., Pss 74:12–17, 93, and, one can argue, 96–99. Language of cosmogony is incorporated into the stories. The cosmogonies *function* like the story of the exodus and land taking. Hence both the stories of the exodus-land taking and the cosmogonies deserve to be called a "national story," since both tell how a nation/people arose.

Though the function of both historical recital and cosmogony in these psalms is the same (to narrate how this people came into existence), they are not purely identical. What are the differences between them? There are two major differences—language and perspective. In psalm cosmogonies (at least in their ideal form) God or the gods are the actors and the language is mythic; they are "stories of the gods" in the nineteenth-century definition of the Grimm brothers. As in the Ugaritic texts, the actors are gods or at least actors on a superhuman level rather than flesh and blood inhabitants of the earth.

To express the relationship between the two levels of activity, I suggest a change in the customary terminology. The term "myth" labors under too many disadvantages to be useful; it connotes untruth in English and moreover implies a dichotomy with history. I propose "suprahistoric" and "historic" and limit the new terms to language and perspective, for the difference between them is mainly one of perspective and language. One must ask from which viewpoint is the story told—of heaven or of earth? Does the narrative focus on the human world or on the divine world, on God or the gods or superhuman actors? My main argument is that the national story can be told in two ideal versions, one historic where emphasis falls on human characters and motivations, and the other

8. These remarks are based upon my "The Hebrew Scriptures and the Theology of Creation," *Theological Studies* 46 (1985) 507–523, and "Creation in the Hebrew Bible," in *Physics. Philosophy and Theology: A Common Quest for Understanding* (ed. R. J. Russell, W. R. Stoeger, and G. V. Coyne; Vatican City: Vatican Observatory, 1988) 151–170.

suprahistoric where the emphasis falls on heavenly beings. The types are ideal; usually there is mixing between the two perspectives.

It is time to test these general observations in the two genres.

A. Communal Laments

A regular feature of the communal lament is a recital of the glorious past, e.g., Pss 44:2–9; 74:12–17; 77:12–21; 80:9–12; 83:10–13; 89:2–38. The recitals have been generally regarded as attempts to highlight the tragedy of the present by contrasting it with the glorious past of the recital.[9] But mere contrast of past and present is not an adequate explanation. It explains neither the length nor the varied details of the recitals. The narrative in Ps 44:2–9 describes Israel entering Canaan as a victorious army led by Yahweh and constitutes a third of the poem. Ps 77:12–21 (counting the invocation) is one half the psalm; it tells of God's redeeming arm, a cosmic battle between Yahweh the God of storm and Sea, Israel's passage through the Sea, and the appointment of Moses and Aaron as leaders. Ps 89:2–38 describes Yahweh's victory over Sea and arrangement of the universe, which climaxes in the installation of the davidic king; it is two-thirds of the lament. Psalm 74 devotes six of its twenty-three verses (vv 12–17) to Yahweh's slaying of Leviathan and orderly arrangement of the world. Ps 80:9–12, the transplanting of the vine Israel from Egypt to Canaan, is a fifth of that psalm. If the psalmists wanted to contrast past glory and present misery they could have done so directly and economically by a simple allusion to the glorious events of the past.

The answer to the question why the psalmists put such artistry into the historical recital can only be that they tailored the recital to the specific lament. Selection of details from the "days of old" differs in each lament according to what is being lamented. Psalm 89, lamenting the defeat of the davidic king by his enemies, recites Yahweh's past sharing the fruits of his cosmogonic victory with David and making him *'elyôn,* "Most

---

9. H. Gunkel, *Einleitung in den Psalmen* (3d ed.; Göttingen: Vandenhoeck & Ruprecht, 1977) 129–30; S. Mowinckel, *The Psalms* (New York: Abingdon, 1967) 1. 196–97, 205; C. Westermann, *The Praise of God in the Psalms* (Richmond: John Knox, 1965) 55–57. The authors see the old saving events as motives to persuade God to act now in like manner but none explains in detail how the particular details of the history are related to the prayer.

High," among the kings of the earth by an unconditional oath.[10] The recital poses a specific question to God: if you unconditionally promised worldwide sovereignty to the davidic line when you made the world, why does your king suffer defeat? Psalm 74 retells Yahweh's ordering of the paired elements of the universe (springs and torrents, land and waters, day and night, moon and sun) that is now threatened by the destruction of the Temple, which commemorates that creation. The question: will you let your enemies destroy the symbol of your creation? Psalm 77, sung by a cantor for a community doubting the ancient promises (vv 8–11), recites the story of Yahweh's superiority over gods and nations, which was once demonstrated by bringing the people through the hostile waters to their land and appointing their leaders. It poses the question: will you let another power annul that founding event? Psalm 44 tells of Yahweh's conquest of the land in order to ask why Israel's enemies rove at will through Canaan.

The recitals of the past in the laments describe not just any period of the past but the moment of origin of Israel: the creation of Israel as Yahweh's people in his land (or shrine) living under his law and leaders.[11] An objection to the proposal must be answered here: if all these psalms speak of one and the same divine act, why has that fact gone generally unrecognized by scholars? Because the act was told in a variety of ways and with different levels of language. The act is variously depicted: the military conquest of Palestine (Psalm 44), the transplanting of a vine (Psalm 80), the defeat of Sea and the appointment of David (Psalm 89), the defeat of Sea and pairing of cosmic elements (Psalm 74), or a march and a cosmic battle (Psalm 77). The language ranges from historic to suprahistoric. Ps 44:2–4 uses ordinary military language to tell how Israel's army conquered Canaan: "O God, we have heard with our own ears; / our ancestors have told us / The deed you did in their days, / with

10. For the unity of this psalm, see R. Clifford, "Psalm 89: A Lament over the Davidic Ruler's Continued Failure," *HTR* 73 (1980) 35–47.

11. "What is 're-presented' are not isolated incidents in history but rather something that had happened which was on-going and all-inclusive, viz., the deliverance at the beginning, as for example in the Credo of Deut. 26 where it is told as a unified story. It is a history which takes place between God and the people. It is to this on-going event that the 're-presentation' of historical events in the Psalms refers, even if only a single event is named" (Claus Westermann, "The 'Re-presentation' of History in the Psalms," in *Praise and Lament in the Psalms* [Atlanta: John Knox, 1981] 246).

your own hand in days of old: / You rooted out nations to plant them, crushed peoples to make room for them. / Not with their own swords did they take the land, / nor did their own arms bring victory; / It was your right hand, your own arm, / the light of your face, for you favored them." The metaphor of (up)rooting in Ps 44:3a is developed in Ps 80:9–17: Yahweh transplants his vine from Egypt to Canaan. Ps 89:6–38, on the other hand, describes "in the beginning" as a battle between Sea personified in Rahab that is followed by a procession of victorious warriors from whom David is chosen and given dominion over earth. The psalm regards the founding of the house of David as part of the foundation of the world just as several Mesopotamian cosmogonies list the king and the temple as things created at the beginning. Ps 74:12–17 similarly takes a suprahistoric perspective. Psalm 77 mixes both perspectives; Moses and Aaron are mentioned (v 21) but so is the cosmic battle between Yahweh as storm God and Sea. Sea is identified with the particular body of water through which Israel passes from Egypt to Canaan. Like Exodus 15, the suprahistoric perspective of the defeat of Sea (which bars the people from their land) is blended with the historic perspective of predominantly human actors, Moses, Aaron, the people, Pharaoh, the Egyptians.

Albertz denies that the primordial conflict depicted in Psalms 74 and 89 is really creation of the world on the grounds that the Baal-Mot and Baal-Yam conflicts in the Ugaritic myths (the source of the psalmic imagery) are not cosmogonies.[12] Albertz *may* be correct in concluding that the Ugaritic texts are not cosmogonies,[13] but he is methodologically wrong in arguing from that evidence that Yahweh's combats with Sea are not cosmogonies.[14] One must argue primarily from the text rather than its

12. Albertz, *Weltschöpfung*, 111–118.

13. Contrary to my view in "Cosmogonies in the Ugaritic Texts and in the Bible," *Or* 53 (1984) 183–201, I now believe that the question whether Baal is a creator-god in the Baal cycle cannot be adequately answered until the general relation of Baal to El is clarified.

14. As correctly noted by Jonas Greenfield, "The Hebrew Bible and Canaanite Literature," *The Literary Guide to the Bible* (ed. R. Alter and F. Kermode; Cambridge: Harvard, 1987) 557. Albertz's dismissal on pp. 112–113 of the cosmogonic combat of Marduk and Tiamat in Enuma elish as late and derivative is an instance of the genetic fallacy, explaining a phenomenon by its origins. As is increasingly recognized, Marduk's combat is not derived from the West Semitic Baal-Yam combat *via* the Amorites but is native, an adaptation of the Anzu myth. Cf. W. G. Lambert, "Ninurta Mythology in the Babylonian Epic of Creation," *Keilschriftliche Literaturen* (XXXIIᵉ Rencontre Assyriologique Internationale; ed. K. Hecker and W. Sommerfeld; Berlin, 1985) 55–60. New Anzu texts (additions to

source. In both Psalms 77 and 89 Yahweh's battle with Sea creates the world of Israel.

Psalm 77 tells of "the wonders of old," the victory of the storm god over cosmic waters that brought Israel as a people into being.

> [16]With your arm you redeemed your people,
>> the descendants of Jacob and Joseph.
>
> [17]The waters saw you, O God,
>> the waters saw you, they were convulsed.
>> Yea, the deep quaked.
>
> [18]The clouds poured forth water,
>> the clouds thundered forth.
>> Yea, the lightning bolts shot to and fro.
>
> [19]The crash of your thunder was in the whirlwind,
>> your lightning lit up the world.
>> the earth quaked and trembled.
>
> [20]In the sea was your way,
>> your path through the mighty waters,
>> your tracks could not be seen.
>
> [21]You led your people like a flock
>> by the hand of Moses and Aaron.

Yahweh uses weapons of thunder and lightning to destroy Sea who had blocked the people from their land. The seemingly abrupt end of the psalm is not really so. By v 21 all the elements constituting a people are in place—god, land, and leaders.

In Psalm 89 the defeat of sea is cosmogonic; it is part of the founding event that includes establishment of the davidic king.[15]

> [2]Your merciful deeds, Yahweh, forever will I sing,
>> Unto all generations my mouth will make known your fidelity.
>
> [3]For you have said, "Forever is (my) steadfast love built,
>> (Like) the heavens is my fidelity established.
>
> [4]I have made a covenant with my chosen one,
>> I have sworn to David my servant.
>
> [5]Forever I will establish your line,
>> I will build unto all generations your throne."

tablets I and III and the complete tablet II) support the inner-Akkadian dependence. Cf. H. W. F. Saggs, *AfO* 33 (1986) 1–29 with comment by W. L. Moran, *AfO* 35 (1988) 24–29.

15. For further details, see my "Psalm 89," 35–47.

Vv 2–38 constitute a single event. The defeat of Sea and ordering of the world (vv 6–15) are followed by a victory procession (vv 16–19) in which one of the warriors, David, is raised up and made "the highest of the kings of the earth." The traditional translation of 'āz in v 20 as "once" is tendentious and contrary to the usual meaning of 'āz in old poetry as "next" or "then."[16] The psalm's main concern is the promise to David in vv 20–38 since it forms such a remarkable contrast to the lament in vv 39–52.

B. The Hymn

The genre of hymn invites the community to praise Yahweh for his deeds on its behalf.[17] The hymn structure is simple: invitatory, the divine action for which praise is to be given (introduced by "for," Hebrew kî), and the repetition of the invitatory. The divine "deeds" or "work(s)" in several psalms are the events that brought Israel into existence, the exodus-land taking, e.g., Pss 66:5–7, 105, 111, 114, 135, 136, and 149. As with communal laments, the events can be described in language that is predominantly cosmogonic, e.g., Psalms 93, 96, and 114.[18] The cosmogonies in these psalms function like the national story, i.e., they are the founding action for which Israel is invited to give praise.

Psalm 136 is a good starting point for the hymn (though a few scholars classify it as a thanksgiving). It praises God for essentially one act—the emergence of Israel as a people in their land. Its version of the founding event is unusually long, incorporating into a single story the making of heaven and earth, the sun, moon, stars (vv 4–9) and the exodus-land taking (from the smiting of the Egyptian first-born to the arrival in the land, vv 10–22). Though many commentators divide the psalm into

16. E.g., Exod 15:15; Jdg 5:8, 11, 13, 19, 22; Pss 2:5; 40:8; 96:12. God selects David through a dream. Promises to a king by means of a vision are common, e.g., 2 Sam 7:4, 17 and 1 Kgs 3:5, 15.

17. A hymn is "the song which extols the glory and greatness of Yahweh as it is revealed in nature and history, and particularly in Israel's history," O. Eissfeldt, *The Old Testament: An Introduction* (New York: Harper, 1965) 105–106, cited in B. W. Anderson, *Out of the Depths: The Psalms Speak to Us Today* (Philadelphia: Fortress, 1983) 134–135.

18. The list is minimal. One could argue for several other psalms that are sometimes classed as hymns, e.g., Psalms 68, 78, 97, 98, 99, 100. The creation hymns 8, 19, and 104 are not discussed here; they treat creation differently; it is not related to the national story.

"creation" and "redemption,"[19] the Hebrew syntax supports no such division. To the psalmist the origin of the people Israel includes the making of the physical environment and the bringing of Israel into the land.

[1]Praise Yahweh for he is good,

. . . .

[4]who alone did great wonders,
[5]who made the heavens through understanding,
 who spread the earth upon the waters,
 who made the great lights,
 the sun to rule the day,
 the moon and the stars to rule the night,
[10]who smote Egypt through their first-born,
[11]who brought out Israel from their midst,

. . . .

[21]and gave their land as a heritage,
[22]a heritage ·to Israel his servant.

Since cosmogonies are usually concerned with the origins of a people it is not surprising that the creation of heaven, earth, and of the sun, moon, and stars, are chapters in the larger story of the rescue of the people from Egypt, their journey through the Red Sea, and their taking of the land. The same logic appears in Psalm 135: the verses "who raises the clouds from the ends of the earth, / makes lightnings for the rain, / brings wind from his storehouses," continue without interruption into "who smote the first-born of Egypt . . ." (vv 7–8). The two psalms tell the story of Israel's emergence as a people; the story is told from both a suprahistoric and historic perspective.

A much more concise example of a single cosmogonic act is Psalm 114. In its dramatically foreshortened perspective, Sea is parallel to the

---

19. G. von Rad is emphatic but not untypical of the tendency: "Verses 5–9 deal with the creation of the world, and at verse ten the psalm abruptly changes its course in order to recount the mighty deeds of Yahweh in history. In this psalm, therefore, the doctrine of creation and the doctrine of redemption stand side by side, yet wholly unrelated the one to the other. Because of the rigid form of the litany, nothing of particular interest emerges from this psalm with regard to the two doctrines which it embraces" ("The Theological Problem of Creation," 133). Cf. H.-J. Kraus, *Psalms 60–150: A Commentary* (Minneapolis: Augsburg, 1989) 498. *NAB* and *NRSV* separate "creation" "redemption" in their stanza divisions; *NJV, REB,* and *NIV* properly make no such division.

Jordan River;[20] Israel goes directly from Egypt to Canaan. The poem is abrupt: there is no invitatory, the third person suffix in v 2 has no antecedent, and the divine name is not even mentioned until v 7. Unmistakable, however, are the allusions to the crossing of the Red Sea and entry into Canaan and to the battle between the storm god and Sea. The latter is found in found in the Ugaritic Baal myth. In *KTU* I.4.7.38–39, Baal's thunder puts his enemies to flight. He utters the taunt: "O enemies of Baal, why do you flee? Why do you flee, O attackers of the Valiant One?" These are the taunts of a heroic age warrior. Sea had attempted to block the entry of Yahweh's people from entering the land and now flees in defeat.

In the hymns examined so far (and also in the communal laments) the key event is not the exodus alone but also the taking of the land of Canaan. The point needs emphasizing because tradition criticism of the Pentateuch has tended to regard the exodus from Egypt and the land taking as separately transmitted traditions that were later woven into a single story. Martin Noth, for example, distinguished five themes in the Pentateuch: the guidance out of Egypt, guidance into the arable land, promise to the patriarchs, guidance in the wilderness, and revelation at Sinai.[21] The distinction is not valid for these psalms. One must speak of an exodus-land taking. Israel's story begins with freedom from Pharaoh's dominion in Egypt and ends with the grant of land in Canaan.[22]

Other hymns make the exodus-land taking the basis for praise, e.g., Psalm 66.

> [5]Come and see the works of God,
>   awesome in the deeds done for us.
> [6]He changed the sea to dry land,
>   through the river they passed on foot.

Psalm 111 defines "the works of the Lord" (v 2) as giving "food to the those who fear you" (v. 5) and "giving [Israel] the lands of the nations"

20. The parallel between Red Sea and Jordan River is made easier by the frequent parallelism of the terms in both Ugaritic and the Bible. Cf. M. Dahood, *Ras Shamra Parallels I* (ed. L. R. Fisher; AnOr 49; Rome: Biblical Institute, 1972) 2. 233, 203, and F. M. Cross, *Canaanite Myth and Hebrew Epic* (Cambridge: Harvard, 1973) 138–139.

21. *A History of Pentateuchal Traditions* (tr. B. W. Anderson; Englewood Cliffs: Prentice-Hall, 1972).

22. A similar point is made by J. Levenson, "Liberation Theology and the Exodus," *Midstream* 35 (1989) 30–36.

(v 6). Psalm 149 makes clear allusion to the Exodus. In all these psalms, the story ends when Israel arrives safely in its land.

In one class of psalms the point is not immediately obvious. In several so-called enthronement psalms, which acclaim Yahweh as universal king, the reason for praise is Yahweh's cosmogony. Universal kingship is based on Yahweh's sole creation of the world. In Psalm 93 the basis for kingship is the victory over Sea that established the world.

> [1]Yahweh reigns, with splendor is he clothed,
>   Yahweh is clothed, is girded with might.
>   The world is founded, it shall never be shaken.
> [2]Your throne is established from of old,
>   From of old you are.
> [3]The Floods lifted up, O Yahweh,
>   The Floods lifted up their roar,
>   The Floods lifted up their pounding waves.
> [4]Mightier than the roar of the Mighty Waters,
>   Mightier than the breakers of Sea,
>   Mighty in heaven is Yahweh
> [5]Your decrees are firmly set,
>   Holiness is fitting to your house,
>   For length of days, O Yahweh!

Yahweh's universal dominion results from his defeat of Floods//Mighty Waters, which would otherwise cover the earth. Once the floods are tamed, Yahweh issues his authoritative decrees (analogous to the *šīmātu* of Mesopotamian cosmogonies) and builds his house. The real interest of the psalm is divine kingship. The cosmogonic victory shows why that kingship is absolute and universal. Other enthronement psalms, one can argue, allude to the same event, e.g., Pss 47:4–5?; 93:3–4; 96:5, 10; 97:2–6; 98:1.

Psalm 33 deals with the theme of creation from another angle. To Albertz, v 5 is a parade example of the polarity between divine majesty, which is found chiefly in praise of the Lord of creation, and divine mercy, which is found chiefly in praise of the Lord of history. "[Yahweh] loves justice" expresses majesty and "of Yahweh's grace is the earth full" expresses goodness.[23] Albertz's polarity between majesty and mercy, creation and history, is a modern distinction; the psalm verses are semantically parallel.

23. *Weltschöpfung,* 91–93.

For Albertz, vv 6–11 develop the first polarity, divine majesty, and vv. 13–19 develop the second polarity, divine mercy.[24] A better interpretation is that vv 6–8 describe God's creation of the biblical three-tiered universe of the heavens, the waters, and the earth. With vv 8–9 the psalmist turns to the third tier, the earth and the human race in order to state the appropriate human response to God as creator. The human race ought to fear the creator God who foils the plots of the nations in order to favor Israel (vv 10–15). Before God's gaze, all human actions except faith and hope effect nothing (vv 16–19). The distinction between creation and history, majesty and mercy, is artificial in the psalm.

For the above hymns, the divine act that is celebrated liturgically is the moment of Israel's origin. It can be described either as the exodus-land taking or as a cosmogony. As with the communal laments, the act can be described ideally from a historic or suprahistoric perspective, or from both perspectives. The mixed perspective invests human history with cosmic significance and God's action with a here and now earthly dimension.

Conclusion

The dichotomy suggested by the terms "myth" and "history" is not valid at least for the story of Israel's origins that is found in several communal laments and hymns. That privileged moment can be narrated from a suprahistoric or historic viewpoint or from a mix of both. The reason that a cosmogony can function as the national story is that ancient cosmogonies customarily included society in the origin of the universe.

If the viewpoint expressed in the above pages has any merit, creation is a much more important theological theme in the psalms than has been previously allowed. It is perhaps possible to show that even more psalms than are mentioned here recite the national story. One might even ask whether the same national story is also the unifying theme of the Pentateuch and thereby establish a link between the Psalter and other parts of the Bible.

24. Ibid.

JAMES L. CRENSHAW

When Form and Content Clash: The Theology of Job 38:1–40:5

The first speech from the tempest presents Job—and all subsequent readers—with a fine example of the collision between literary form and its religious content.[1] One can hardly say that in this instance the medium is the message, for the singular function of theophany,[2] the bringing near of the one who until now has dwelt in concealment, clashes with the content of the speech, the shattering of every human illusion of occupying a special place in God's sight.[3] In examining this remarkable text, I shall address three issues: (1) the logic of the argument attributed to Yahweh; (2) the appropriateness of the subject matter in context; (3) and the theological significance of the divine speech, together with Job's response to it.

1. For a study of this phenomenon in the book of Proverbs, see my essay entitled "Clanging Symbols," *Justice and the Holy: Essays in Honor of Walter Harrelson* (ed. D. A. Knight and P. J. Paris; Atlanta: Scholars, 1989) 51–64.

2. Perhaps this clash is built into the very essence of theophany in the ancient world, particularly because of its close association with natural phenomena and warrior ideology. On the one hand, the manifestation of awesome natural forces elicited terror in persons who witnessed a theophany. On the other hand, the martial imagery ordinarily implied that the deity had come to bestow assistance on the one favored by divine unveiling.

3. Several interpreters have made this point, none quite so emphatically as R. Gordis in *The Book of God and Man* (Chicago and London: University of Chicago, 1965) and, for popular consumption, D. Neiman, *The Book of Job* (Jerusalem: Massada, 1972), who frequently writes about the human illusion of the central position.

70

The Logic of the Argument

In his dispute with the three friends Job levels two fundamental charges against the God whom he has faithfully served. First, God fails to govern the universe properly, that is, in such a manner that virtuous people thrive and wicked individuals come to grief. Second, at the very least God is guilty of criminal negligence.[4]

By placing himself under an oath of innocence[5] and daring to state the dreadful content of individual punishments, Job hopes to compel God to appear in court and defend the divine conduct.[6] If Job is guilty, the curses will crush him, but if innocent, he will escape unscathed and the verdict of guilt will point in another direction. The onus will then fall on God's shoulders to prove divine innocence in the face of weighty evidence to the contrary. It thus appears that Job has seized the initiative and gained the upper hand in the debate.

That impression explains the disappointment often acknowledged over the speeches from the tempest. This discomfiture takes various forms. From a pastoral perspective, a verbose lecture on cosmogony, meteorology, and zoology seems strange comfort for one whose soul aches as a result of personal isolation and loss of family, possessions, and honor. From a legal perspective, the threefold interrogation—did you witness? do you know? are you able?—shifts the focus from the accused and transforms Job into the unfortunate object of calumny. From a literary perspective, the nature wisdom skirts the profound questions being explored, specifically "Does disinterested righteousness exist?" and "How can one explain undeserved suffering?"

---

4. T. N. D. Mettinger, *In Search of God* (Philadelphia: Fortress, 1988) 175–200, offers a recent assessment of these accusations and emphasizes the move from a hidden God (*Deus absconditus*) to a present one (*Deus praesens*). N. Habel, *The Book of Job* (OTL; Philadelphia: Westminster, 1985) 528, writes: "Job's heroic faith has provoked the *deus absconditus* into becoming the *deus revelatus,* even before Sinai."

5. G. Fohrer, "The Righteous Man in Job 31," *Essays in Old Testament Ethics* (ed. J. L. Crenshaw and J. T. Willis; New York: Ktav, 1974) 1–21, underscores the complex manner in which the poet uses a wisdom form to suggest tension between the claim of inner purity and the presence of hybris as well.

6. Various critics have stressed the legal metaphor in the book, most notably H. Richter, *Studien zu Hiob* (ThA 11; Berlin: Evangelische Verlagsanstalt, 1959) and S. H. Scholnick, "The Meaning of *mišpāṭ* in the Book of Job," *JBL* 101 (1982) 521–29, and *Lawsuit Drama in the Book of Job* (unpub. Ph.D. Diss., Brandeis, 1975).

In truth, the opening and closing references in the zoological section
to the violent preying on weaker victims amount to bold admission that
in the animal world the strong survive at the expense of the weak. The
lioness and raven provide for their own; from aloft the hawk and vulture
search for food so that their young may be gorged with blood. In this
world "might makes right," if one may justifiably introduce the subject
of justice at all. The implication that power alone lights up God's eyes
can hardly escape Job's notice, but does that principle operate in the human
realm too?

It would seem so, on the basis of the entire divine speech. Dismissing
the previous debate (Job's? Elihu's?) with a flick of the hand, God orders
Job to prepare for intellectual combat,[7] at the same time echoing Job's
earlier curse on the day an announcement declared the birth of a boy
(literally—geber, 3:3). The one who presumed to challenge the creator
listens as God asks if he were present at the birth of land and sea, light
and darkness (38:4–21). This evocation of certain features of the creation myth leaves virtually no room for chaos to exercise any threat
whatever.[8] The emphasis falls on God's design and control over the
elements. Job was not present when the creator laid earth's foundations,
determined its dimensions, measured it exactly and set its cornerstone
in place. Nothing is left to chance here, and festive celebration by a celestial
choir accompanied the completion of the building.

Then God supervised the birth of the sea, mentioned here because this
turbulent water symbolized chaos in ancient myth. After clothing its unruly
waves in dense cloud, Yahweh restricts the sea's domain by a powerladen
decree. Having secured the earth on its pillars, God moves on to single
out light from darkness (Sheol), asking Job if he has ever commanded
dawn to take hold of earth's fringes and to shake out the denizens of
wickedness like vermin in a blanket[9] or if he has descended to the

7. C. Gordon understands the imagery differently. For him, Yahweh uses an allusion
to belt wrestling (HUCA 23 [1950–51] 131–36).

8. J. D. Levenson, Creation and the Persistence of Evil (San Francisco: Harper and
Row, 1988) discovers various degrees of opposition to Yahweh in the several accounts of
creation within the Hebrew Bible and attempts to place these different traditions on a
temporal continuum. All such efforts, however ingenious, are rendered dubious by the
likelihood that the views derive from competing guardians of the tradition about creation, some of whom may have lived at the same time.

9. The NEB (and REB) indicate the difficulty presented by this text, which may actually
contain a reference to a constellation rather than to wickedness.

Underworld and learned the secrets of death and its realm.[10] The operative word here is certainly "power," but a subtle hint implies that God somehow attends to the problem of controlling wickedness, concentrated in nocturnal activity, and the suggestion of definite order in the universe moves far beyond mere hinting. The question about Job's ability to conquer evil advances by degrees as the speeches progress—from human wickedness to natural evil, symbolized by Behemoth, and supernatural evil, personified in Leviathan.[11]

Yahweh's references to cosmogony conclude with ironic mockery of Job's brief existence, then a shift to discussion of meteorology occurs (38:22–38). Here, too, a curious ambivalence surfaces, for Yahweh claims that hail is reserved for the time of warfare. Neither here nor in the earlier allusion to shaking wicked ones out of the horizon does one find any assurance based on the sort of calculating morality that permeates the arguments in the dispute. Furthermore, God emphasizes the impartiality of life-giving rain, which falls on terrain as yet undisturbed by human feet. Throughout this section, the imagery of generation and parturition seems to echo Job's earlier complaint about his own conception and birth.[12] Job's inability to command the constellations, order lightning to do his bidding, or channel the rain for his own ends merely underscores his utter helplessness in mastering the rules that govern the heavens.

The section on zoology restricts itself to wild animals, with the notable exception of the mighty war horse, which excites the Lord greatly. Besides the aforementioned violent creatures, the following beasts parade before Job in splendid formation: the mountain goat, the wild doe, the wild ass, the wild ox, the ostrich, the horse, the hippopotamus, the crocodile. Yahweh questions Job about the sexual habits of goat and deer, asking if he serves as midwife to them, and about the freedom of ass and ox, inquiring whether he can tame them for domestic service. The description of the ostrich draws on popular lore about its stupidity, curiously

10. Behind this allusion may rest a rich tradition about descent into the Underworld, one that is illuminated nicely by texts from Mesopotamia. We cannot be sure how much familiarity with this myth the author of Job had.

11. This distinction between Behemoth and Leviathan may press the symbolism excessively. In any event, the restrained language encourages caution with respect to the necessity for talking about mythic creatures here. In my view, the animals are real, but they conjure up images of beasts from the realm of myth.

12. R. Alter, *The Art of Biblical Poetry* (New York: Basic Books, 1985) 99. Alter's insights on the relationship between chapter 3 and the divine speeches are fresh and compelling.

referring to God in the third person,[13] and affirming that God denies wisdom to this strange creature who can outrun horse and rider. The second divine speech continues this zoological description, turning first to the hippopotamus and concluding with the crocodile. At the outset, however, God challenges Job to accomplish a feat that even the deity seems to find daunting, namely abasing proud human beings.

The divine argument possesses a certain kind of logic, one suggested by the creation myth and by Job's radical attack on that event concentrated in his own birth. Cosmogony, meteorology, and zoology constitute the mythic liturgical tradition as seen in the Priestly account, while one searches the speeches in vain for the other creation tradition, the fashioning of men and women.[14] This missing datum is surely no accident, for the absence of any human being at creation gives resounding testimony to Job's littleness. In the whole speech God makes only a casual allusion to a rider astride a mighty steed. Still, Job could derive some comfort from the fact that he is being addressed by the creator, even though both the mode of speech and its content betray a spirit of mockery.[15]

Perhaps Job could also find solace in Yahweh's refusal to offer simple solutions to complex questions, for gain in access to life's mystery could only come at the expense of forgoing the condition of human existence. The most one can do is discover an analogous situation, to wit that suffering and evil belong in the category with the unknown and unknowable, like the origins of the universe and the marvelous instincts of creatures over whom human beings exercise no control. Moreover, Job could derive

13. The same phenomenon occurs in more than one place where the Hebrew text alludes to the punishment of Sodom and Gomorrah. Although God is represented as the speaker, a shift takes place to refer to Elohim in the third person as instigator of the calamity (cf. Amos 4:11).

14. R. Albertz, *Weltschöpfung und Menschenschöpfung: Untersucht bei Deuterojesaja, Hiob und in den Psalmen* (Calwer Theologische Monographien 3; Stuttgart: Calwer, 1974) develops this distinction as it applies to the book of Job, while P. Doll, *Menschenschöpfung und Weltschöpfung in der alttestamentlichen Weisheit* (SBS 117; Stuttgart: Katholisches Bibelwerk, 1985) extends the discussion to include Proverbs as well.

15. Gerhard von Rad, *Wisdom in Israel* (Nashville and New York: Abingdon, 1972) 225, writes: "All commentators find the divine speech highly scandalous, in so far as it bypasses completely Job's particular concerns, and because in it Yahweh in no way condescends to any kind of self-interpretation." L. Alonso-Schökel, "God's Answer to Job," *Job and the Silence of God* (ed. C. Duquoc and C. Floristan; New York: Paulist, 1983) 45, cites interesting examples of comments by scandalized interpreters.

confidence from the assurance that God has created the world in a way that allows every creature to develop according to its nature,[16] although one's place in the pecking order would surely temper that confidence.

The Appropriateness of the Content

One expects that Lord to respond to Job' s charges and to demonstrate their falsity, thus exonerating the deity. We remember, however, that the Prologue has Yahweh concede that the adversary has incited the Lord to strike out against a loyal servant without cause. Nevertheless, the divine speech will have none of this willingness to accept responsibility for Job's misery. Instead, Yahweh labels Job a faultfinder and accuses him of obscuring the divine design of things by ignorant talk. It appears that the prologue also prepares us for the possibility of two divine speeches, analogous to the twofold unfolding of calamity and Job's response to each affliction.[17] If this is correct, one may legitimately conclude that the two speeches address the two charges leveled at the deity.

Recent interpreters have emphasized the cogency of the two speeches as responses to Job's charges that the universe lacks order and that God is a criminal.[18] In their view, the first speech denies the accusation of criminality and the second speech addresses the matter of divine governance of things. The first argument is a subtle one; the Lord implies that the creator who watches over every creature and provides daily sustenance can scarcely be guilty of cruelty toward any living thing. If anything, this solicitous ruler actually deserves the title of "Bountiful Provider," for God

16. According to L. E. Goodman, Saadiah explains the divine speeches in terms of three conceptual themes: (1) the pure grace of creation; (2) the constitution of natures in things; and (3) the provision of each creature with its own niche (*The Book of Theodicy* [Yale Judaica Series 25; New Haven and London: Yale University, 1988]).

17. On one reading of the book, Job's initial confession (1:21) gives way to one that contains considerable ambiguity (2:10). Similarly, the first response to the divine speeches expresses ambiguity (40:4–5) and the final one returns to the confessional stance (42:2–6). This neat *a b b' a'* pattern is broken by the presence of great uncertainty as to the meaning in the last words of Job.

18. O. Keel, *Jahwes Entgegnung an Ijob: Eine Deutung von Ijob 38–41 vor dem Hintergrund der Zeitgenössischen Bildkunst* (Göttingen: Vandenhoeck & Ruprecht, 1978) and V. Kubina, *Die Gottesreden im Buche Hiob* (Freiburg: Herder, 1979). The latter author's emphasis on the historical dimension of the divine speeches lacks persuasiveness.

dispenses largesse without regard to need or merit, indeed pours out precious rain on uninhabited soil.

It seems to me that this initial speech also addresses the charge that God presides over a chaotic world, for in describing the creation of the world Yahweh uses language of precise measurement, secure foundations, and cornerstones. The same point is made differently when Yahweh claims to have laid a statute on the sea, commandments on the morning, and ordinances on the heavens. In Yahweh's view, even the rain has channels and lightning has paths, while snow and hail are held in abeyance until their proper time.

Such language about Yahweh's complete control over the created order is every bit as effective in responding to the issue of a chaotic world as the second speech. There Yahweh launches an attack on Job, challenging him to overcome all human pride and to conquer all wickedness.

Are we to deduce from this description of things the slightest concession that Yahweh faces a task that even the sovereign creator finds to be at best difficult? If so, this monumental concession must be viewed in the light of the extraordinary ease with which the Lord overcomes the symbolic forces of evil, Behemoth and Leviathan. The choice of these two beasts can hardly be accidental, for their mythic role in the Egyptian worldview illuminates the description in chapters 40–41 wonderfully.[19] Even the forces of evil are subject to their creator's will, Yahweh insists, and mighty Behemoth enjoys special status because of temporal priority. Leviathan, too, stands as king over all proud creatures. Job's puny darts have bounced off the Lord like human missiles hurled at the powerful crocodile, who must surely symbolize deity in this context.[20]

It thus seems likely that the two divine speeches respond *after a fashion* to the two accusations Job has leveled against God, but the deity's silence with respect to the significant issues of the book other than the forensic ones strikes many readers as strange. In one sense the divine speeches utter sublime irrelevance, for they offer no insight into the fundamental existential dilemma confronting Job. What conceivable justification exists

19. Keel, *Jahwes Entgegnung an Ijob.*
20. J. T. Wilcox, *The Bitterness of Job* (Ann Arbor: University of Michigan, 1989) thinks the speeches celebrate certain aspects of fertility religion, evoking in Job a renewed appreciation for the sexual. The evidence Wilcox adduces is not very convincing to me, especially the conclusions based on the names Job gives to his daughters.

for human suffering, particularly undeserved suffering? More to the point, how should one respond to innocent suffering?

The author of the book has certainly shown little reticence about offering various traditional understandings of suffering, merited or otherwise: it comes as punishment for wickedness; as disciplinary warning; as a test intended to expose or to shape true character; as a means of purifying one's innermost being; it will vanish when God acts; it reveals hidden truth, human and divine. The poet's silence about suffering in the divine speeches probably amounts to an admission that none of these explanations satisfactorily unveils the mystery of suffering. If the poet, wisely, we think, refrained from offering a simple answer for ultimate mystery, that is still no reason for failing to offer guidelines on how human beings ought to respond during undeserved suffering.[21]

Perhaps the speeches and Job's reluctant responses do say something important with regard to the proper way to behave during suffering. The difficulty lies in the ambiguity of Job's responses. The first answer, forced on him by a persistent deity, emphasizes Job's insignificance, his lightweight status in competing in a heavyweight arena. The use of an expression for smallness contrasts with the weightiness of the Lord,[22] but how should one understand the concession? If I am so worthless, what can I answer?[23] Because of my littleness, what shall I say? In other words, is this response tantamount to a refusal to concede the dispute? This reading actually paves the way for a second divine speech, which aims at eliciting a more acceptable response from Job.

Unfortunately, the second response continues the ambiguity of the first.[24] Does Job reject his legal claim, his attack on God, his God, himself,

21. The contrast with the Mesopotamian composition "I Will Praise the Lord of Wisdom" is noteworthy, for this text emphasizes liturgical remedies for affliction, constituting the whole thing a paradigm of an answered lament.

22. The Hebrew word *qallôtî* implies that Yahweh's speech has certainly impressed Job with his puny stature when compared with the mighty creator whose honor (*kābôd*), although challenged, was still heavy indeed.

23. J. G. Janzen, *Job* (Atlanta: John Knox, 1985) 243, understands the opening word *hēn* as "if" rather than "behold." W. L. Michel, *Job in the Light of Northwest Semitic* (BeO 42; Rome: Biblical Institute, 1987), 1. 95, interprets 4:18 and probably 15:15 and 25:6 the same way (i.e., *hēn* as "if").

24. C. Muenchow, "Dust and Dirt in Job 42:6," *JBL* 108 (1989) 597–611, endeavors to throw light on the difficult text by appealing to the sociocultural milieu in which the book was written.

his repentance? Does he melt, abase himself, and derive comfort from his ritual acts? Or does Job maintain his rebellion to the end? What does he mean by dismissing all previous experience of God as derivative in favor of immediate sight? We do not know the answers to these important questions. Thus far the text of the theophany has emphasized speech, remaining completely silent about the actual form which the poet imagines God to have assumed. Why, then, does Job give voice to such daring confession? Has his hope of vindication become reality? After all, he claims to have stood before God with impunity (13:16), indeed to have beheld deity and survived. If Job has been vindicated, his speech in 42:6 may properly signal final acquiescence, a willing surrender before divine majesty.

Subtle changes occur even when the two Joban responses and God's immediate challenge to Job that he offer an answer cite earlier language. At first Job is accused of obscuring (literally, "darkening") the design imposed on the universe by its creator (38:2), whereas later in the text God uses the image of concealing the divine plan of things (42:3). Even within the first divine speech, God's language varies when urging Job to respond. In 38:4 Yahweh orders him to declare if he knows "understanding" (*bînâ*), but 38:18 has "Declare if you know all of it" (*kullāh*).

What about the question attributed to the adversary as the decisive issue under discussion: "Will anyone serve God for nothing in return?" The speeches from the storm ignore this question altogether. Does the poet assume that Job's confessions of trust and submission within the prose settle this matter once and for all time? That can hardly be true, for Job quickly alters that position in the dialogue. One could possibly interpret the divine speeches as indirect response to the question about disinterested righteousness. They imply that the abundance of divine favor, indeed its almost wasteful excess, leaves no room for human claims to serve God without thought of reward. Grace comes to all creatures in such superfluity that the matter of merit can find no place of entry.[25] Accordingly, all creatures owe their very existence to a generous deity. Such an understanding of the text presses it to the limit, particularly in light of what appears to be divine badgering of Job.

This point raises the issue of God's rhetoric. Often characterized as excessive, bombastic, nagging, and the like, this constant belittling of

25. This point occurs often in Saadiah's commentary on Job (*The Book of Theodicy*), esp. p. 360; but note also Goodman's introductory comment on p. 37.

a hurting creature may reflect an educational setting, if the harsh treatment of students by their teachers in Mesopotamia and in Egypt permits one to assume that the author of Job knew this phenomenon and used his knowledge to good effect.[26] Furthermore, the choice of medium for the divine appearance seems especially cruel, given the earlier mention of a tempest in the prose.[27] Curiously, the breakthrough in the story about the theophany to Elijah on Mt. Horeb does not express itself within the sapiential resort to revelation through a special appearance of the deity.[28] Must the poet convey the impression of power regardless of the consequences?

Although the interrogative form of the divine speeches reduces adult questions to the status of schoolroom exams, this choice of questioning has been called an essential veil for presenting ideas worthy of deity.[29] In prophetic literature the supposed enigmatic character of divine oracles functioned similarly to erect an imaginary wall between ordinary discourse and transcendent speech. This point can be pushed too far, for the hymnic passages in the dialogue and in Elihu's address closely resemble the divine speeches, and prophetic literature teems with oracular speech that makes no apology for attributing the views to God.

Perhaps the questioning form functions in yet another way—to shift the emphasis from Job's goodness to his knowledge. As long as the issue pertained to Job's virtue, no one could fault him, for in the prose even God bore witness to his singular character.[30] Therefore, the questions

26. On ancient pedagogy, see my essays entitled "Education in Ancient Israel," *JBL* 104 (1985) 601–15, and "The Acquisition of Knowledge in Israelite Wisdom Literature," *Word and World* 7 (1987) 245–52.

27. The actual words differ, *rûaḥ gĕdôlâ* in 1:19, *sĕ'ārâ* in 38:1.

28. If critics are right in assuming that wisdom literature normally limits itself to observable phenomena, this resort to theophany is astonishing, as is Eliphaz' earlier description. Perhaps it is better to acknowledge different forms of wisdom, in one of which present revelation plays a significant role. In another form, revelation took place at creation when the deity locked secrets of the universal order in the cosmos and left them there for human discovery at some subsequent time. In any event, one would expect sages to stress communication by means of an inner still voice rather than one associated with great commotion.

29. M. Tsevat, "The Meaning of the Book of Job," *Studies in Ancient Israelite Wisdom* (ed. J. L. Crenshaw; New York: Ktav, 1976) 341–74, insists that the solution to the book must have *intellectual* content. For him, the God who turns to Job is neither just nor unjust but God. Why then does Job say, "My eye sees *you*"?

30. Some literary critics would assert that an even more unimpeachable source, the omniscient narrator, attests to Job's purity (1:22; 2:10).

in Yahweh's speeches draw attention away from Job's exemplary conduct to his partial knowledge. Consequently, some interpreters take note of the fact that Job's flaw existed in the cognitive domain (e.g., Maimonides, Aquinas). In their view, he was a good man with only partial knowledge. After all, he does confess that he was ignorant prior to the divine revelation, which replaced rumor with first-hand experience. Such a way of formulating the discovery of fresh insight strikes one as peculiar in an ethos that normally highlighted hearing as the way new information was acquired.[31]

Theological Significance of the Speeches

Interpreters have consistently seen the book of Job as a radical challenge of traditional views about the relationship between act and consequence.[32] They have not been quick to recognize that the divine speeches constitute an equally radical criticism of the anthropocentric presupposition of ancient sages.[33] Human hybris bursts before this rapturous celebration of a universe in which women and men play no role other than that of awestruck witness to grandeur and terror. On the one hand, Job challenges the view of God as benevolent creator, insisting that the deity is both malicious and hidden. On the other hand, the poet has Yahweh express genuine excitement over creatures who strike terror in humans. Job's parody of Psalm 8 pales in comparison with the Lord's virtual silence about humankind.

This revolutionary perspective occurs with amazing poetic restraint. We read simply, "Then Yahweh answered Job from the tempest" (38:1). No elaboration of Yahweh's appearance, no reference to accompanying seraphs or cherubs, no stress on the inadequacy of linguistic representation of deity can be found here. The poet does not even try to defend the use of a genre that belongs to liturgical traditions more readily than

31. The conclusion to Ptahhotep has a fine word play that develops this aural aspect of learning at great length, but the same emphasis on hearing occurs widely in wisdom literature where instruction often took the form of oral recitation.

32. L. Boström, *The God of the Sages* (CB 29; Lund: Almqvist and Wiksell, 1990) 90, characterizes the relationship as character-consequence rather than act-consequence.

33. M. Sekine, "Schöpfung und Erlösung im Buche Hiob," *BZAW* 77 (1958) 213–23, emphasizes the manner in which the divine speeches take Job back to primordial times in order to actualize his redemption in the present.

to sapiential ones. The language of theophany is reported in a matter of fact way; the extraordinary has become ordinary.[34] Such restraint contrasts sharply with the actual content of the divine speeches, where rhetorical flourish abounds.

Not only do the divine speeches demolish human pride. They also reveal a problem for what it is, a mystery.[35] The intellectual and religious quandary becomes even more perplexing after the divine input, for the partial answers that the poet exposes in the prose and dialogue have not taken into account the complexity of the universe as unveiled by its maker. In a sense, the poet has Yahweh announce the collapse of the sapiential enterprise,[36] for the human intellect cannot guarantee wellbeing in the kind of world that Yahweh parades before a chastened Job. Perhaps the introduction of a theophany into the book of Job functions to convey this awareness of wisdom's ultimate ineffectiveness. When confronted by a problem, the intellect knows almost no limit, but the situation changes drastically once mystery enters the picture. Problems are susceptible to solutions; mysteries can only be illuminated. We exercise control over problems, whereas mystery seizes us and generates in us a sense of wonder.

The claim that Yahweh speaks and resolves the book's intellectual probing poses a special kind of problem. For obvious reasons, religious people tend to grant more authority to the Lord's words than to mere human speech.[37] Naturally, the poet gave a privileged position to Yahweh for precisely this reason. What happens, however, when views attributed to God cause embarrassment of one kind or another? In this instance, Yahweh's description of the ostrich preserves folklore that does not coincide with actual reality. When this strange creature abandons her eggs—or

34. The effects, however, of this divine manifestation are far from ordinary, even if Job refuses to cower in fear before his accuser.

35. G. Fohrer, "Dialog und Kommunikation im Buche Hiob," *Studien zum Buche Hiob (1956–1979)* (BZAW 159; Berlin and New York: de Gruyter, 1983) 135–46. G. Gutiérrez, *On Job* (Maryknoll, New York: Orbis, 1985) xviii, also thinks silence is central to the mystery of God, but the problem of the book, as he sees it, concerns proper speaking about God in suffering.

36. B. Vawter, *Job and Jonah* (New York: Paulist, 1983) 86: "Wisdom, philosophy, in other words, is pronounced a dead end. . . . The God of the theophany of Job is a *deus absconditus* even more remote than the God on whom Job refused to call."

37. The search for the exact words of God in prophetic criticism of a recent era was undoubtedly fueled by such an assumption, as if removing all glosses placed one in the presence of authentic revelation.

her young—she does so to lure predators away from her brood. This point illustrates a fundamental problem associated with scripture, namely, the tendency to confuse human words with divine communication.[38] That mistake worsens as a result of the literary fiction of divine speech.

Another problem about the book has immense theological significance. Job's responses to his calamities and to the speeches from the tempest use terribly ambiguous language. Does that fact suggest that human response to deity inevitably bears a doublesidedness? That, because life unfolds in such obscure fashion, men and women hedge their bets? Faced with one whose power can crush him in a second, does Job resort to verbal ambiguity and hope that Yahweh will fail to recognize the shady nuance?[39] The difficulty with this detection of irony in Job's response is that it ignores the sages' belief that God saw into the depths of human hearts. Such duplicity on Job's part would not have escaped Yahweh's sight, in the sages' view. Therefore, the ambiguity must result from poetic ineptness, which is unlikely, or it must function theologically to acknowledge that all divine-human encounter is cloaked in ambiguity. The very assertion that human beings enjoy such high status as addressees of transcendence is subject to counter claim or outright denial—hence the necessity for language that suggests the tenuousness of the situation.

This observation leads to a general point about the metaphorical nature of all theological discourse. As is well known, all language about God is necessarily symbolic; we use metaphors because we wish to describe the unknown in terms of the known. In the end, however, we succeed only in fashioning fragile stained-glass windows[40] through which we behold our own images of ultimate reality. No human being will ever know whether or not those images correspond with anything in the transcendent realm, for that certainty would require one to forfeit the condition of finitude.

38. Red-letter editions of the Bible foster this illusion that one has access to Jesus' actual speech, glossing over the fact that those words passed through extensive theological shaping at the hands of early Christian theologians.

39. Some such assumption characterizes those interpreters who view Job's response as ironical, for example, J. G. Williams, "'You Have Not Spoken Truth of Me': Mystery and Irony in Job," ZAW 83 (1971) 231–55, and "Deciphering the Unspoken: The Theophany of Job," HUCA 49 (1978) 59–72.

40. "God is above and beyond; the images and symbols should remain what they are: not solid prison walls, but the fragile stained-glass windows of transcendence" (Mettinger, In Search of God, 207).

Having said that, I hasten to add that the text depicts an ambiguous sovereign, one who can best be described by means of two metaphors, creator and warrior.[41] The first is obvious, the second less so. Yet the elusive references to the presence of recalcitrant forces in the world despite Yahweh's immense power justifies the adoption of the image of the Lord as one who continues to engage the forces of evil in combat.[42] Astonishingly, the traditional symbols of chaotic powers, Behemoth and Leviathan, seem to pose less of a threat than does human pride. In this ongoing battle, the Lord enlists Job's assistance,[43] but acknowledges that the task is beyond human achievement. Then does the text imply that eventual victory over evil will come through divine agency? Such an apocalyptic reading of the crucial verse (38:23) offers more hope than the text seems to suggest.

Indeed, the total impression left by reading the book of Job conveys little comfort. The God of the prologue yields to manipulation, and despite confidence in at least one exemplary human being acquiesces in a set of events that leaves havoc in its wake. What is more, this deity expresses no dismay over wanton destruction of life and property, although complaining about being incited to afflict a favorite servant without cause. The deity of the epilogue waxes hot against Job's three friends, who must surely have offered the best answers to Job's suffering that they could muster. Moreover, this God bestows favor on Job once more and replaces his lost children as if this action makes all things right. Even if this restoration of Job does not fall into the category of reward for something,[44] whether integrity or intercessory prayer, it has certainly struck many interpreters as odd.

The depiction of God in the poetry is equally troubling. The friend's

41. It may be more accurate to conflate these metaphors, for the imagery of battle is inherent to a full expression of the idea of creation.

42. In the Prolegomenon to my *Studies in Ancient Israelite Wisdom,* I call attention to the continuing conflict between God and chaos, a point that Levenson, *Creation and the Persistence of Evil,* skillfully develops.

43. Perhaps this interpretation of God's challenge to Job bestows far more dignity on the human subject than the text allows, for the point certainly highlights Job's inability to overcome pride in himself or in others.

44. Most interpreters have understood the restoration of Job as reward for faithfulness, which contrasts with the lying words of the three friends, according to the perspective articulated in the epilogue. One can conceivably view the restoration as further sign of divine munificence that does not take merit into account.

understanding of God removes the deity from the human scene, save for terrifying moments, and separates mortals from their creator by a chasm so vast that human deeds count for nothing. Elihu's disciplinary God is a little more palatable, although in the end Elihu also envisions a supreme and remote being untouched by human frailty or accomplishments. At the other end of the spectrum, Job's God presents two faces, [45] malevolence and absence. Readers who expect the divine speeches to bring relief from this litany of undesirable divine attributes are disappointed. If anything, the portrayal of deity in the speeches increases the distance between human beings and their maker. This distancing takes place, paradoxically, despite a literary form that emphasizes incredible closeness. Here form and content clash, with the latter gaining supremacy. Must "the greater glory of God" always require a belittling of human beings?[46]

45. C. Westermann, "The Two Faces of Job," *Job and the Silence of God*, 15–22, discusses the analogous contrasting descriptions of God's servant Job.

46. For the theological elucidation of this point, see my introduction to *Theodicy in the Old Testament* (Philadelphia and London: Fortress and SPCK, 1983) 1–16. By taking the theophany as normative, we conclude with Wilcox that "the book as a whole is profoundly skeptical, agnostic; its message is largely a counsel of silence" (Wilcox, *The Bitterness of Job*, 122).

GALE A. YEE

The Theology of Creation in Proverbs 8:22–31

This paper will examine the theology of creation as it is found in a fundamental Wisdom text, Prov 8:22–31. The language used by our author is highly metaphorical, employing analogies from human experience to articulate the essentially incomprehensible nature of God and of God's relationship with human beings. As the primary linguistic means through which we conceptualize Deity, metaphors by their very nature cannot define God; they cannot and should not be taken literally. On the flip side of the metaphorical coin of "God is" is the deconstructive assertion that "God is not."[1] For Sallie McFague, metaphors are principally adverbial, having to do with how we *relate* to God, rather than defining the nature of God's self.[2] The creation theology in Prov 8:22–31 conceptualizes the relationship of humanity with God through Wisdom, whereby the metaphors of this relationship are of the procreative and creative God with God's daughter Wisdom, as well as Wisdom's own co-creative relationship with humanity.

1. The deconstructive character of metaphor has been overlooked or ignored by some male scholars who, in reaction to feminist works, defend an exclusively male language for God: R. M. Frye, "Language for God and Feminist Language: Problems and Principles," *SJT* 41 (1988) 441–69, esp. 462–68; J. W. Miller, "Depatriarchalizing God in Biblical Interpretation: A Critique," *CBQ* 48 (1986) 609–16; and "In Defense of Monotheistic Father Religion," *Journal of Religion and Health* 21 (1982) 62–67.

2. S. McFague, *Models of God: Theology for an Ecological, Nuclear Age* (Philadelphia: Fortress, 1987) 39, and also *Metaphorical Theology: Models of God in Religious Language* (Philadelphia: Fortress, 1982) 1–29.

The Literary Context of Prov 8:22–31

In my previous work on the 'iššâ zārâ (foreign woman),[3] I situated Proverbs 8 in the context of speeches delivered by different characters throughout Proverbs 1–9. The framework of these speeches is as follows:

	Prov 1:11–14	Speech of the Sinners	A
	Prov 1:22–33	Speech of Wisdom	B
	Warning vs. the 'iššâ zārâ—2:16–19		
I	Prov 4:4–9	Speech of the Father's Father	B'
	Warning vs. the zārâ—5:1–11, 15–23		
	Prov 5:12–14	Speech of the Son	A'
	Warning vs. the 'ēšet rā'—6:23–35		
	Prov 7:14–20	Speech of the 'iššâ zārâ	A
	Prov 8:4–36	Speech of Wisdom	B
II	Prov 9:5–6	Speech of Wisdom	B'
	Prov 9:16–17	Speech of the 'ēšet kĕsîlût	A'

These speeches are set within the overall instruction of the father to his son in Proverbs 1–9 and are intended to be heuristic devices through which the father makes his point. They divide themselves into two main groups that form two chiastic patterns. In both groupings the speeches of Wisdom and her spokesperson (viz., the father's own father in 4:4–9) are far longer than those of the sinners, the misled son, and the 'iššâ zārâ. Even in literary quantity the speeches of Wisdom and her agent outweigh the rival group, thus highlighting the veracity of their claims. Furthermore, the chiastic structure highlights the speeches of Wisdom and her agent in each of the two groups (B/B').

In this framework, the person of the foreign woman becomes the very antithesis of Woman Wisdom. The author characterizes the two as competitors for the same man: the son instructed by the father. Both women are described in dangerously similar terms; both utter perilously similar messages to beckon the young man to their respective houses. In the first chiastic group of speeches the 'iššâ zārâ does not speak. Instead, she appears in the repeated warnings of the father to his son to keep far away from her (2:16–19; 5:1–11, 15–23; 6:23–35). In second chiastic group of

3. G. A. Yee, "'I Have Perfumed My Bed with Myrrh': The Foreign Woman ('iššâ zārâ) in Proverbs 1–9," *JSOT* 43 (1989) 53–68.

speeches, she is given voice in 7:14–20 where she herself verbalizes the dangers she presents to the ignorant son.

Wisdom's speech in Proverbs 8 is situated structurally to refute the parallel discourse of the 'iššâ zārâ in Proverbs 7. Addressing the same population as the 'iššâ zārâ, viz., the simple and foolish (8:4–5; cf. 7:7 and 9:16), Wisdom makes seemingly fantastic claims. In contrast to her competitor, Wisdom speaks of what is right and true (8:6). Her instruction is worth more than silver, gold, or jewels (8:10–11, 18–21). Kings and leaders rule through her (8:14–16). Those who seek her (and not the 'iššâ zārâ; cf. 7:7–8) will find her and will be blessed with a genuine love (and not the adulterous love that the 'iššâ zārâ offers; cf. 7:13–20).

As we shall see, Wisdom, to justify her indispensable worth to humanity, expounds on her beginnings in 8:22–31, setting herself in opposition to the 'iššâ zārâ. The origins of the latter are *foreign*. Her very alienage becomes a metaphor for the disruption of the social order of the created world, leading to death itself.[4] In complete contrast, the origins of Wisdom are from God before and during the creative ordering of the world itself. Her intimate relationship to God as daughter becomes a metaphor for the Divine's continuing presence in the social order, leading to life itself.[5]

Metaphors of Creation in Prov 8:22–31

In another article devoted to Prov 8:22–31, I examined the internal development of the poem to show how its structure and rhetorical features conveyed meaning and purpose.[6] The table from this article is reproduced in the following:

4. C. V. Camp, *Wisdom and the Feminine in the Book of Proverbs* (Sheffield: Almond, 1985) 120 and, "Wise and Strange: An Interpretation of the Female Imagery in Proverbs in Light of Trickster Mythology," *Semeia* 42 (1988) 19–22. In "What's So Strange About the Strange Woman?" in *The Bible and the Politics of Exegesis* (ed. D. Jobling, P. L. Day, G. T. Sheppard; Cleveland: Pilgrim, 1991) 17–31, Camp argues that the strange woman is a male metaphor for the socio-political disruptions of familial and social stability in a post-exilic context.

5. A full-scale critique of the patriarchal symbolization of evil in female form in Proverbs 1–9 is beyond the scope of this essay. Instead, see C. A. Newsom, "Woman and the Discourse of Patriarchal Wisdom: A Study of Proverbs 1–9," in *Gender and Difference in Ancient Israel* (ed. P. L. Day; Minneapolis: Fortress, 1989) 142–60, and the provocative analysis of the 'iššâ zārâ by C. Camp, "Wise and Strange," 14–36, cited in n. 4 above.

6. G. A. Yee, "An Analysis of Prov 8:22–31 According to Style and Structure," *ZAW* 94 (1982) 58–66.

Proverbs 8:22–31

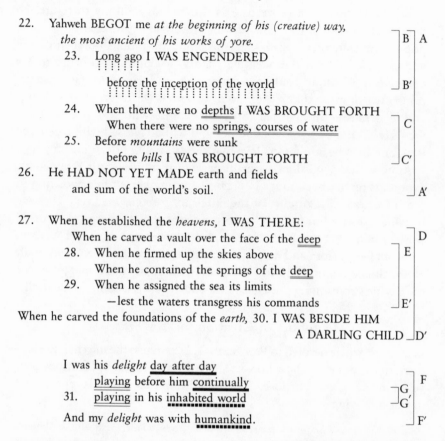

22. Yahweh BEGOT me *at the beginning of his (creative) way,*
    the most ancient of his works of yore.
    23.   Long ago I WAS ENGENDERED

           before the inception of the world
    24.   When there were no depths I WAS BROUGHT FORTH
           When there were no springs, courses of water
    25.   Before *mountains* were sunk
           before *hills* I WAS BROUGHT FORTH
26. He HAD NOT YET MADE earth and fields
    and sum of the world's soil.

27. When he established the *heavens,* I WAS THERE:
    When he carved a vault over the face of the deep
    28.   When he firmed up the skies above
           When he contained the springs of the deep
    29.   When he assigned the sea its limits
           — lest the waters transgress his commands
When he carved the foundations of the *earth,* 30. I WAS BESIDE HIM
                                   A DARLING CHILD

    I was his *delight* day after day
           playing before him continually
    31.   playing in his inhabited world
    And my *delight* was with humankind.

The poem is divided into three strophes, delineated by stichs A/A′, D/D′, and F/F′ at the far right. The stichs of each strophe are indicated in the column left of the strophe column. The basic poetic technique in the hymn is *parallelismus membrorum.* Not only does our author use simple parallelism of two cola within a particular stich but also distant antithetical parallel pairs which form *inclusiones,* so to speak, framing A/A′ and D/D′. The final third strophe climaxes the poem through a chiasmus punctuated by alliteration.

I saw a progression in the hymn which this tri-strophic structure accentuates. Wisdom's privileged position began when she was begotten by God before the creation of the world (Strophe A/A'). Wisdom was beside God as a darling child, when God created the world and carefully insured its safety from the chaotic waters that threaten to engulf it (Strophe D/D'). The chiasmus in Strophe F/F' structurally highlights Wisdom's mediative role between God and humanity. Wisdom was God's playful delight (F) and her own delight was with humanity (F').

As I reexamine the poem again to determine its theology of creation, I keep in mind what I discussed above regarding metaphor. I am concerned about the metaphors the author uses to describe not only the creation of the world but also the Creator God, Wisdom, and humanity. I am concerned with the quality of *relationship* among these agents which these metaphors convey adverbially. Finally, I am concerned about the adequacy of these biblical metaphors for our time.

In Prov 8:22–31, I see three major metaphors for the Deity forming an affilial matrix with the metaphors of Wisdom, humanity, and the world. The three metaphors, God as procreator, God as creator, God as co-creator and re-creator, will be used to structure the following discussion. Although I am keeping these three metaphors of God analytically distinct, they are, as we will discover, very much interdependent.

God as Procreator

In Strophe A/A' Wisdom describes her origins through metaphors of birthing: she was begotten (B),[7] engendered like a fetus (B'),[8] brought

---

7. While the usual meaning of the root *qnh* is "to buy or acquire," the verb is used in Gen 4:1, Deut 32:6, and Ps 139:13 where the parenting aspect is evident. See W. A. Irwin, "Where Shall Wisdom Be Found?" *JBL* 80 (1961) 133–42, for the most thorough argument for *qnh* as "to beget." Also, see M. Dahood, "Proverbs 8,22–31: Translation and Commentary," *CBQ* 30 (1968) 512–21; B. Lang, *Wisdom and the Book of Proverbs. A Hebrew Goddess Redefined* (New York: Pilgrim, 1986) 63–65; and Camp, *Wisdom and the Feminine,* 306 n. 7. For a different opinion, consult B. Vawter, "Prov 8:22: Wisdom and Creation," *JBL* 99 (1980) 205–16 and, "Yahweh: Lord of the Heavens and the Earth," *CBQ* 48 (1986) 461–67.

8. I accept the BH emendation *nĕsakkōtî* from the root *skk,* which appears to be a form of *nsk.* The root *skk* occurs in two striking instances. In Ps 139:13 the psalmist states that he was woven in the womb of his mother. In Job 10:11 Job reminds God that God had knit him together with bones and sinews. The process of gestation in both cases is described metaphorically in terms of a craft. Moreover, in Ps 139:13 *qnh* parallels *skk,* the same situation as our present text, Prov 8:22–23.

forth in labor (C/C'). Her birth "at the beginning" (A) structurally contrasts the fact that God had not yet made the totality of the created world
(A').[9] Wisdom *was born* before the creation of the world. While metaphors
of the Wisdom's origin are those of birth, the metaphors describing the
creation of the world in Strophe D/D' are those of construction and building.[10] Thus the origin of Wisdom is envisioned metaphorically as comparable to that of human beings themselves.[11] Her beginning is not only
temporally but also qualitatively distinct from the rest of the created world.

The metaphors of birth underscore Wisdom's relationship to God as
daughter. How does the text picture God's relationship to Wisdom? The
metaphors of birth imagine a procreating God. In the realm of human
experience, the act of procreation involves two sexes, male and female.
While the root *qnh* can describe both sexes,[12] *skk* and especially the double
use of *ḥll* tip the scale in favor of the female depiction of God here.[13]
My concern with our text, however, is not to insist on the gender of God
which is beyond our comprehension, but on the metaphorical way in
which God's relationship to Wisdom is envisioned and its ramifications
for a creation theology.

I approach the matter of the God-Wisdom relationship by pointing
out along with other scholars that the figure of Wisdom is a personification. A personification is a type of metaphor that calls attention to the
unity of its subject. In our case, the personification of the abstract noun
Wisdom calls attention to the unity of "wisdoms" which it represents
and for which it speaks.[14] Woman Wisdom not only personifies God's
own wisdom but also the human wisdom tradition itself. Divine and
human wisdom find their unity in the personification of Woman Wisdom.
Sustaining this mysterious unity, Woman Wisdom represents divine
immanence in the created world of humanity. She is revelatory of God
as well as of the human capacity to try to understand this God in the
created world.[15]

9. Yee, "Analysis of Prov 8:22–31," 62–63.

10. God establishes, carves, firms up, contains, and assigns the rest of creation in
vv 27–29.

11. A. Berlin, "Motif and Creativity in Biblical Poetry," *Prooftexts* 3 (1983) 235.

12. See the discussion of Irwin, "Where Shall Wisdom Be Found," 137, on the Ugaritic
evidence where *qny* describes both El and Asherah.

13. Camp, *Wisdom and the Feminine*, 306 n. 7.

14. Ibid., 214–15.

15. C. Camp, "Woman Wisdom as Root Metaphor: A Theological Consideration,"

Another important fact is that this personification of God's own wisdom and human wisdom is embodied in a female figure. Claudia Camp has convincingly argued that the specifically female figure became an authoritative religious symbol in the kingless society of the post-exilic period. Woman Wisdom exemplified God's wisdom, seen in the wisdom of subtlety and indirection characteristic of women at that time. Female wisdom was based on the home, replacing the court wisdom of a society ruled by a king.[16]

In Strophe A/A' this female personification of divine and human wisdom is given birth by a procreating God. Emphasized here through this metaphor is the intimacy that will be shared between the Deity and the created social order through Wisdom. While the Deity still preserves transcendence, God will be manifested in the created world through the birthing of God's daughter before the creation of this world. On the one hand, Wisdom begotten by God partakes of the Divine itself. On the other hand, she is autonomous from God (as a child is from its parent), as she is beside God in the creation of the world, playing among humanity.

I am not suggesting here that Wisdom becomes an hypostasis that would compromise the monotheism of the Hebrew faith.[17] Woman Wisdom functions as a literary device personifying the abstract concept of Hebrew wisdom. This wisdom is seen as the mysterious communion between divine and human wisdom which was discernible in the created world order. This wisdom originates from God's very self, articulated in Strophe A/A' as being procreated by God. Wisdom is manifested in created reality, pictured in Strophes D/D' and F/F' where Woman Wisdom is beside God in the creation of the world and ultimately plays within this created world.

God as Creator

The metaphors of God creating the world in Strophe D/D' are those of building and construction: God establishes (D), carves, firms up (E),

---

The Listening Heart: Essays in Honor of Roland E. Murphy (ed. K. Hoglund, et al.; Sheffield: JSOT, 1987) 58–59; R. E. Murphy, "Wisdom—Theses and Hypotheses," *Israelite Wisdom: Theological and Literary Essays in Honor of Samuel Terrien* (ed. John Gammie, et al.; Missoula: Scholars Press, 1978) 38–39; and, "Wisdom and Creation," *JBL* 104 (1985) 9–10.

16. See Chapters 8 and 9 of Camp, *Wisdom and the Feminine*, 233–91.

17. Cf. the concerns of R. Marcus, "On Biblical Hypostases of Wisdom," *HUCA* 23 (1950–1951) 167–71.

contains, assigned limits (E′), carves (D′). I argued in my previous work that the adverb *šām* qualifying *'ānî* in v 27 is made more precise in v 30a by *wā'eheyeh 'eṣlô 'āmûn,* forming distant parallel stichs framing the second strophe with the antithetical fixed pair "heaven" and "earth." The structure of the strophe artistically highlights the metaphor of Woman Wisdom who, during all this activity, is beside the creator God as a darling child (D/D′).[18]

Strophe D/D′ contains a thematic progression in God's construction of the world from what is above to what is below. Stichs D and E concern themselves with the creation of the upper cosmos: God establishes the heavens, carves a vault over the face of the deep, and firms up the skies above. Stichs D′ and E′ describe the ordering of the lower dimensions of the world: God carves the foundation of the earth, contains the springs of the deep and assigns the sea its limits. Creation here is not of the physical cosmos for its own sake. Richard Clifford has argued that ancient Semitic cosmogonies do not view the "world" that emerges from creation by the gods simply as the physical planet. Rather,

> it is the world of men and women living in a defined land, secure from enemies, with social and culture systems well established. The order which the cosmogonies describe is the benign arrangement of the elemental forces to support human life.[19]

The imagery of construction in Strophe D/D′ thus reveals a divine purpose: from top to bottom God is taking care to secure the safety the world for Wisdom and humanity from hostile forces. This purposeful ordering particularly becomes clear in the clause in E′, *ûmayim lō' ya'abrû pîw,* "lest the waters transgress his commands." The preoccupation with the waters of the deep reflects the beliefs found in ancient Semitic myths

---

18. See Yee, "An Analysis of Prov 8:22–31," 63–64. I have made an exegetical choice to read the MT *'āmôn* as *'āmûn,* "little child or ward" in order to be consistent with the parent/child metaphor. Some have related *'āmôn* with the Akkadian *ummānu,* "craftsperson, scribe, counselor," modifying God or Wisdom herself. J. C. Greenfield argues that the description of Wisdom as counselor ties in with the earlier description of her in Prov 8:1–21 as an adviser to kings and princes, and a source of truth and justice ("The Seven Pillars of Wisdom [Prov. 9:1]—a Mistranslation," *JQR* 76 [1985] 17–18).

19. R. J. Clifford, "Cosmogonies in the Ugaritic Texts and in the Bible," *Or* 53 (1984) 201. See also J. L. Crenshaw, "Prolegomenon," *Studies in Ancient Israelite Wisdom* (ed. J. L. Crenshaw; New York: Ktav, 1976) 26–31.

that the primeval oceans continually menace the created world from above and from below.[20] It is from these chaotic waters that the creator God secures the safety of the world.

The image of God as creator in Strophe D/D' should not be divorced from that of God as procreator in Strophe A/A'. God does not simply beget Wisdom and then set about creating the world. The whole progression of this strophe reveals several truths: the protective and nurturing labors of God the parent in insuring the safety of the world for Wisdom and humanity against the chaotic oceans antagonistic to it, the power of God the parent in keeping these waters at bay, and above all else, that during these achievements, Wisdom was at God's side, a darling child. The creation theology that emerges in our text is one where the procreating God begets Wisdom and builds a home for her, protecting and nurturing her growth in this created world.

God as Co-creator and Recreator

The metaphor of Woman Wisdom in the climactic strophe F/F' is of a child at play. The strophe is chiastically structured in the interplay between *ša'ašu'îm* "delight" and *měśaheqet* "playing." The chiasmus structurally highlights Wisdom's mediative role: Wisdom is the delight of God the parent (F/G); her own delight is in God's inhabited world with human beings (G'/F').[21]

There are two clues to this strophe's creation theology, one temporal, the other attitudinal. One finds the first clue in the adverbs describing Wisdom's joyful activity: "day after day" and "continually." Creation is the divine establishment of order in the cosmos for the purposeful existence of human beings and other living things. Since this order must be maintained, creation is not a once-for-all event but a process taking place continually.[22] Forces, personified in Wisdom's nemesis, the *'iššâ zārâ*, continually threaten to disrupt the social order. The context of 8:22–31 within Proverbs 8 as a whole reveals Wisdom's call to all humanity

---

20. Cf. Gen 1:2, 7; Pss 74:12–17; 104:6–9, 24–26; Job 38:8–11.

21. Yee, "An Analysis of Prov 8:22–31," 65.

22. Cf. H.-J. Hermisson, "Observations on the Creation Theology in Wisdom," *Israelite Wisdom: Theological and Literary Essays in Honor of Samuel Terrien* (ed. John Gammie et al.; Missoula: Scholars Press, 1978) 46–47.

to heed her voice and not that of the foreign woman. Indeed, Wisdom proclaims:

> I have good advice and sound wisdom:
>> I have insight, I have strength.
> By me kings reign
>> and rulers decree what is just. (8:14–15)

Through the mediation of Woman Wisdom (the personification of divine and human wisdom), God and humanity become co-creators in the ongoing task of keeping the created world order stable.

The second clue to this strophe's creation theology is the metaphor of play describing Wisdom. Some scholars are disturbed with the metaphors of birth and play in the poem. They think that the image of a gay, thoughtless child is inappropriate in the context of the verses prior to and following Prov 8:22–31 that summon the foolish and simple to heed her.[23] According to Camp, however,

> Play is a fundamentally liminal deconstructive activity. For Wisdom, it takes place at the heart of the interaction between God and humans, and, thus, at the heart of the theological endeavor.[24]

Context determines the ways in which play is a "fundamentally liminal deconstructive activity." In some contexts, play indeed can be frivolous and careless, but this is not the case here. For one thing, *God* delights or recreates in the play of Wisdom (F). Play characterizes the *relationship* between God the parent and Wisdom, stressing the intimacy of that relationship. It is this intimacy with God the parent that grounds Wisdom's authority in her appeal to humanity, vis-à-vis the *'iššâ zārâ*.

Second, the conditions of play between parent and child are total love, happiness, trust, and a freedom from fear and hardship. It is precisely this security from hostile forces that was established by God the parent in creating a home for Wisdom. The play and delight of both parties is the exuberant acknowledgment of the safety and order of the created world which makes this play possible.

Third, play characterizes the *relationship* between Wisdom and humanity (F'). Play is that posture of joy and wonder before creation in women

23. Cf. R. B. Y. Scott, "Wisdom in Creation: The *'Āmôn* of Proverbs VIII 30," *VT* 10 (1960) 218–19.

24. Camp, "Woman Wisdom as Root Metaphor," 61.

and men who seek Wisdom. It is an aesthetic perspective toward the cosmos that dispels an attitude of mere use or senseless exploitation of it. It exhilarates implicitly in the safety and order of the universe that God first made possible. In "wise" adults this play is tempered with the thought that in order for this play to continue to happen, they must be co-creators with God in maintaining the divine order and stability of the created world.

The Theology of Creation in Prov 8:22–31

There are advantages in approaching Prov 8:22–31 metaphorically. The first is that the conceptualization of God is inclusive. God is seen as male, female, and even neither. God is fundamentally a parent in all that this means. Furthermore, the image of the parent gives purpose and meaning to the mixing of creation metaphors in the text: those of birthing, those of construction, and those of play. The metaphors of God as builder of the world become clearer when one carries over the birth metaphor into the creation of a secure home for the child, and the happiness and play of both the parent and the child once a sense of security is achieved.

The particular model of a procreating God begetting divine/human wisdom has three benefits for a creation theology: "it brings us closest to the beginnings of life, to the nurture of life, and to the impartial fulfillment of life."[25] We have seen these three in the structural development of Prov 8:22–31.

As I stated above, the origin of Wisdom is envisioned metaphorically as comparable to human beings themselves. The power of the metaphor lies in the fact that the closest encounter human beings have with the mystery of creation is the birth of new life from their bodies. The human capacity for divine wisdom finds a very powerful model in the procreating God. The image underscores the intimacy wise human beings have with God through Wisdom. In their co-creative task, this divine/human wisdom is also begotten in and through their bodies as it is passed on, generation after generation, through their children.

As God labored to build an ordered stable home for Wisdom that she may not only survive but grow to maturity, so too do human parents

---

25. McFague, *Models of God,* 104.

nurture and guide to fulfillment those whom they bring into existence, at tremendous physical, economic, and emotional costs. The wise raise their children and others under their care in and through Wisdom, instilling within them the goodness of creation through which they will find God and imparting to them a sense of responsibility to preserve that goodness.

In both their procreative and creative gifts, human beings become co-creators with God in the continual process of keeping the world secure. The moments celebrating the gift of life and its preservation, the awe and wonder at creation, are those of play. The wise know and understand that these moments are only possible through their efforts in Wisdom. In an age where the threat of ecological and nuclear extinction is upon us, it is incumbent on the wise to insure for their own generation that this play can happen for the next. In a time when life itself is endangered, Wisdom's words at the end of Proverbs 8 become ominously prophetic:

> The one who finds me finds life
>   and obtains favor from the Lord;
> But those who miss me injure themselves;
>   all who hate me love death. (8:35–36)

MICHAEL KOLARCIK

Creation and Salvation
in the Book of Wisdom

In a recent work, Pierre Gibert studied the development of "creation
theology" in the Old Testament.[1] Two features of this work have a bearing on clarifying the Wisdom author's understanding of creation: a) the
first is the cross-referencing of allusions between the stories of creation
in Genesis (P) and the stories of the exodus event; b) the second is the
historical development evidenced in the creation accounts which are based
on the three cultural contexts of Canaan, Babylon, and Hellenism.

The first feature is well known.[2] The Priestly account of creation, which
stresses the ordering of the world through division, affirms a victory over
chaos parallel to the victory of God over Israelite slavery at the hands
of Pharaoh's forces. Conversely, the separation of the sea in the escape
of the Israelites alludes to the victory over the primeval waters as well
as to the mastering of cosmic forces through division and separation.
Creation is understood as a type of liberation, and the Exodus is understood as a form of creation.

The second feature is more complex. Three accounts of creation are
analyzed in Gibert's work with respect to the intentionality of the story
and to the language which the account employs. Each creation account
is marked by the milieu in which it was formulated: 1) Genesis 2–3

1. P. Gibert, *Bible, mythes et récits de commencement* (Parole de Dieu; Paris: Seuil, 1986).

2. Other recent works that have stressed the common language and allusions between
the Exodus event and the Priestly creation account are found in J. L. Ska, *Le passage
de la mer* (AnBib 109; Rome: Biblical Institute, 1986); Paul Beachamp, *L'un et l'autre Testament* (2 vols.; Parole de Dieu; Paris: Seuil, 1976, 1990).

[Canaanite], 2) Genesis 1 [Babylonian], 3) 2 Maccabees 7 [Hellenistic]. The stories of Adam and Eve (Genesis 2–3) function as a summary of the fundamental experiences of the human predicament. Genesis 1 employs language that highlights the dependence of creation on the word of God. Finally, 2 Maccabees 7 is a confession of faith that reduces to its barest elements the biblical treatment of creation: the explicit recognition of the radical impossibility of "grasping" origins, while simultaneously confessing God as the origin.[3]

Gibert's assertion that the philosophical precision of Hellenism (exemplified in the example of 2 Maccabees) helped creation theology to crystallize its "barest elements" may well be a valid one with respect to the use of mythical language.[4] However, there is another phenomenon at work in the creation theology of Israel's Hellenistic period, that is particularly evident in the Wisdom of Solomon. Both Creation and the Exodus become paradigms for understanding salvation which culminates in apocalyptic. The apocalypse, an ultimate judgment, is viewed as the culmination of the creative forces of the cosmos which save, liberate, and reward the just.

For the Wisdom author, creation, exodus, and salvation are all related as signs of God's justice and goodness. Therefore, all three signs are related through a common set of terms and imagery. It is the cosmos that functions as a constant in the references to creation, to the exodus event, and to the apocalyptic judgment.[5] By attributing a creative and wholesome

3. "I do not know how you came into being in my womb. It was not I who gave you life and breath, nor I who set in order the elements within each of you. Therefore the Creator of the world, who shaped the beginning of humankind, will in his mercy give life and breath back to you again, since you now forget yourselves for the sake of his laws" (2 Macc 7:22–23).

4. No doubt it appears rather strange for an exegete to focus on creation theology in the Hellenistic period without attention to a major contribution of the sapiential tradition to creation theology, namely the personification of wisdom. For reasons of specialization and limitation of the field of inquiry, Gibert limits the passages under consideration (*Bible, mythes et récits de commencement,* 141, 151). Nonetheless, the unique perspective of creation theology of the Wisdom author does not consist in the "barest elements" of faith in God, the creator, but rather in the continuity of creation in history which culminates in apocalyptic.

For a detailed overview of the figure of personified wisdom in the Book of Wisdom and its relation to the Hellenistic version of the Isis cult, see J. S. Kloppenborg, "Isis and Sophia in the Book of Wisdom," *HTR* 75 (1982) 57–84.

5. J. J. Collins has noted the consistency of the Wisdom author's employment of the creative function of the cosmos in the three major sections of the book ("Cosmos and

role to the cosmos in creation, in the exodus events, and in the ultimate judgment, the author points to the continuity of creation in the history of Israel's faith. The exodus event and the ultimate judgment are the continuity of God's creative efforts. Both events reestablish God's goodness and justice through an overcoming of chaos and a destruction of injustice.

Each major section of the Book of Wisdom (first—chapters 1–6, second—chapters 7–10, third—chapters 11–19) contributes a unique perspective to this unity within its creation theology.

1) Wis 1:1–6:21: The Creative Role of the Cosmos in the Ultimate Judgment

The first section of the Book of Wisdom (1–6) consists of an exhortation to justice which focuses its attention on dissuading the reader from bringing on death through injustice (1:12–16; 2:21–24). Death, understood by the author as an intrusion into the cosmos, is the prime negative image for eliciting the pursuit of virtue and justice. Within the unfolding of the argument through the metaphor of a trial scene, the apocalyptic judgment of chapter 5 functions as the sentencing, the vindication of the just and the destruction of wickedness. In the two extreme contexts within this argument, namely that of the first creation and of the ultimate judgment, the author emphasizes the creative role of the cosmos.[6]

Salvation: Jewish Wisdom and Apocalyptic in the Hellenistic Age," *HR* 17 [1977] 128). "It appears then that the Wisdom of Solomon presents a coherent theology throughout the book. God is encountered through the cosmos, by wisdom. History illustrates the structure of the universe, and eschatology is also built into that structure. The human way to salvation is by understanding the structure of the universe and adapting to it in righteousness."

6. The first six chapters of Wisdom form an elegant concentric structure which both highlights the similarities between units and emphasizes their differences. 1:1–15, an exhortation to justice which dissuades the reader from choosing death, is parallel to 6:1–21, an exhortation to wisdom in order to be just. 1:16–2:24, the wicked's defense for their choice of power and injustice is parallel to 5:1–23, the wicked's confession of error. The central unit 3:1–4:20, consists of four parallel diptychs through which the author disproves the wicked's defense and defends the integrity of the just. The first detailed presentation of this literary structure is in A. G. Wright, "The Structure of the Book of Wisdom," *Bib* 48 (1967) 165–84. For a complete presentation of the concentric structure, see M. Gilbert, "Sagesse de Salomon (ou livre de la Sagesse)," *DBSup* 11 (1986) cols. 114–19, or M. Kolarcik, *The Ambiguity of Death in the Book of Wisdom 1–6* (AnBib 127; Rome: PBI, 1991) 50–62.

The author feels compelled to discuss the relationship between the death that God did not make and the cosmos which God did create. It is here that the author emphasizes the beneficial aspect of all the creatures and forces of the cosmos in perhaps the most unequivocal terms in all of Scripture. The beneficial feature of creation is a key principle in the author's creation theology. Verse 1:14 stresses the wholesome aspect of creation first through two positive statements which are followed by two negative declarations.[7]

> For God created all things to be,
> and the forces of the world are wholesome,
> (καὶ σωτήριοι αἱ γενέσεις τοῦ κόσμου)
> and there is no destructive poison in them,
> nor is the dominion of Hades on earth (1:14).

With such emphasis on the healthy aspect of the world in the opening clarifications on creation, it is not surprising to see the author attribute to the cosmos a prime role during the ultimate judgment which re-establishes justice (5:17–23).[8] This second principle is a consequence of

7. The author's statements in 1:14 are as remarkable as their images are difficult to interpret. The precise deciphering of the statements' connotations and allusions remains elusive. Certainly, the author's idea of the generative forces being wholesome is consistent with Philo of Alexandria's notion of the perpetuity of the species (Philo, *Quis rerum divinarum heres,* 118, 159). Similarly, Philo's exclusion of evil forces from matter (ibid., 315–16) echo the Wisdom author's negative image of destructive poison (φάρμαχον ὀλέθρου), which likewise is excluded from the forces of the cosmos. Perhaps the exclusion of destructive poison from the forces of the cosmos also includes a polemic against Egyptian beliefs as postulated in their version of the Isis cult with its cosmological suppositions (in contrast to the Hellenistic version). Isis is presented as a magical healer against destructive forces in the world (see Kloppenborg, "Isis and Sophia in the Book of Wisdom," 79–83). For a thorough treatment of the possible allusions and interpretations of 1:14, see also C. Larcher, *Le Livre de la Sagesse ou la Sagesse de Salomon* (EBib Nouvelle série; Paris: Cerf, 1983–1985) 202–6.

8. This analogy of arming the cosmos through the metaphor of a hoplite's armor is an adaptation of Isa 59:17–19. The author of Wisdom has tightened the analogy by comparing divine zeal to the armor of a hoplite (instead of to the divine mantle as in Isaiah) and then by identifying each weapon with a moral attribute. However the Wisdom author's major adaptation of the analogy in Isaiah is the expansion of the idea that the cosmos itself is armed to do battle against wickedness. There is only a hint of the elements of the cosmos in the metaphors of a "rushing stream" and the "wind" in Isa 59:19. See M. J. Suggs, "Wisdom of Solomon II, 10–V: A Homily Based on the Fourth Servant Song," *JBL* 76 (1957) 28–33; Kolarcik, *The Ambiguity of Death in the Book of Wisdom 1–6,* 47, 106–7.

the first. Since the cosmos is beneficial and wholesome, then it works on the side of God to reward the just and destroy wickedness.

As a result of the confession of the wicked among one another in Wis 5:1–14, the setting is prepared for judgment to be executed in favor of the just and against the wicked. God re-establishes justice by calling upon creation itself which is in alliance with God and justice.

> 5:17 The Lord will arm creation (τὴν κτίσιν) as a defense against enemies.
>
> 5:20 The cosmos (ὁ κόσμος) will fight with God against the demented.

In the apocalyptic scene that follows, the elements of the cosmos (lightning, hailstones, waters of the sea, a mighty wind), wreak havoc on lawlessness, an ethical chaos (ἀνομία, κακοπραγία). For the author of Wisdom, these elements of the cosmos allude both to the original creation which overcomes chaos and to the exodus events where, as we shall see in the last section of Wisdom, the elements transform themselves do battle against Israel's enemy.

In this first section of Wisdom, the author has drawn a direct parallel between the original creation of God where the cosmos is emphasized as being wholesome, and the ultimate judgment where God re-establishes justice by overcoming ethical chaos as if in a renewed creation. These relations of creation and the ultimate judgment to the cosmos form two key principles operative in the author's creation theology. 1) The cosmos is wholesome and just because God has created it, and 2) the function of the cosmos is to continue the work of creation by helping the just and by destroying lawlessness.

In the presentation of the ultimate judgment, the author has brought the reader to the lofty heights of a divine perspective where the realities of blessedness and moral tragedy stand clearly over against the appearance of the power of injustice and the impotence of virtue. But what basis is there for the author to construct this sure hope in an ultimate judgment which completes the original creation? The basis for this perspective is elaborated in the following sections of Wisdom. There the author roots the hope in an ultimate judgment on the concrete history of the world's salvation, and specifically the salvation of the Israelites in the exodus.

2) Wis 6:22–10:21: Creation is Parallel to Salvation through Wisdom

If the first part of Wisdom can be understood as the author's exhortation to justice by a dissuasion from following a life of injustice that leads to death, the second part of Wisdom (6:22–10:21) can be grasped as the author's exhortation to wisdom by a presentation of the positive attributes and gifts of God's wisdom in the cosmos. The first is a dissuasion from death; the second is a persuasion to life. By means of the personified figure of wisdom, the author joins together God's original creation to the continuous recreation of God in salvation history.

The speaker throughout these chapters is the unnamed figure of Solomon who appreciates the limitations of his human condition and the need for God's wisdom that comes from on high (7:1-9). Unlike the wicked in the first section (2:1–5), Solomon understands the fragile human condition to be open to divine wisdom. For the wicked in chapter 2, the transience of human life was judged to be final and tragic. As a result of their disparaging judgment on the mortal condition of humans, they considered power, injustice and even sheer violence to be viable options in this passing world (2:6–20). Whatever is weak they judged to be useless. Instead of giving in to despair as the wicked, Solomon prays for the wisdom that comes from God. What encloses the famous prayer for wisdom in chapter 9 is the presence of wisdom in creation (9:1–3) and in salvation (9:18).[9] God has created humanity through wisdom, and it is through wisdom that humanity is continuously saved.

> O God of my ancestors and Lord of mercy,
> who have made (ποιήσας) all things by your word
> and *by your wisdom* have formed (κατασκευάσας) humankind[10]

---

9. The prayer for wisdom in chapter 9 is formulated in a concise concentric structure. See M. Gilbert, "La structure de la prière de Salomon (Sg 9)," *Bib* 51 (1970) 301–31.

$$
\begin{array}{ll}
a\ 9{:}1{-}3 & a'\ 18 \\
\quad b\ 4 & \quad b'\ 17b \\
\qquad c\ 5{-}6 & \qquad c'\ 13{-}17a \\
\qquad\quad d\ 7{-}8 & \qquad\quad d'\ 12 \\
\qquad\qquad e\ 9 & e'\ 10b{-}11 \\
\qquad\qquad\quad f\ 10a
\end{array}
$$

10. This opening verse of the prayer of Solomon duplicates the double notion of creation in Genesis 1; that is, the creation of the cosmos and of humanity. However, it would

> to have dominion over the creatures you have made
> and to rule the world in holiness (9:1–3) . . .

> And thus the paths of those on earth were set right
> and people were taught what pleases you,
> and were saved (ἐσώθησαν) *by wisdom* (9:18).

The linkage between creation and salvation is emphatically explained in the central part of the prayer. Since wisdom was present when the world was made, she knows the hidden plans and ways of God in the world.

> With you is wisdom, she who knows your works and was present
> when you made the world (ὅτε ἐποίεις τὸν κόσμον);
> she understands what is pleasing in your sight
> and what is right according to your commandments (9:9).

It is this relationship between God and wisdom, at the time of creation, that the author uses to explain the continuous effort of wisdom to bring humanity back onto the paths of creation.

Salvation, for the author of Wisdom, is understood as God's effort to bring humanity to the point of realizing the original intentions at creation. Therefore, it is through the gift of wisdom, who was present at creation, that the unnamed Solomon will be guided wisely (9:11), whose works will be acceptable and who will be able to judge justly (9:12). Solomon will be able to put into practice the intention of the creator through the gift of wisdom who was present at creation.

This feature of wisdom's function to save humanity by virtue of her role in creation is elaborated in examples from the Pentateuch. Beginning with Adam and ending with Moses (Wisdom 10), the author recounts how, at critical moments in the history of humanity, wisdom intervened on behalf of humans to restore and save the just.[11] On the other hand,

---

be incorrect to separate the creation of the cosmos from the creation of humanity within the author's presentation. They are presented together as a continuum, just as the Genesis 1 creation account exemplifies. There is no underlying idea present here of a creation of the cosmos that is separate from the creation of humanity.

11. Adam is contrasted to Cain, 10:1–3; Noah is contrasted to those who perished in the flood, 10:4; Abraham is contrasted to the nations who were put into confusion (Babel), 10:5; Lot is contrasted to those who perished in the cities of the plain and even to his wife, 10:6–8; Jacob is contrasted first to Esau, 10:9–10, and then to Laban and personal enemies 10:11–12; Joseph is contrasted to his brothers and to Potiphar's wife,

those who practiced injustice and who fled from wisdom perished.

By relating wisdom's saving activity to her presence at creation, the author of Wisdom focuses the lens of creation theology to view the salvation history of Israel. Each saving moment is a recreation. Wisdom saves because she was present at creation and therefore knows how to restore the conditions of creation for the just. The last and brief contrast between the Israelites and the Egyptians at the end of chapter 10, leads the author to begin the final developed presentation. The exodus is re-interpreted as the privileged moment of salvation. This interpretation of the exodus reaffirms the feasibility of postulating an ultimate judgment and serves as the paradigm of salvation — God's recreation of the world in favor of the just.

3) Wisdom 11–19: The Exodus Is Presented as the Primary Example of Salvation Where Creation Itself Is Transformed[12]

In the opening section of Wisdom, the ultimate judgment was presented through a series of declarations. The author chose to depict the scene of judgment through imagery that alludes to creation, wherein the cosmos itself is armed to reward the just and to destroy moral chaos. But how is this assertion for an ultimate judgment feasible in the author's argumentation? The entire reasoning process of the author to disprove the false judgment of the wicked in chapter 2 rests on the postulation of an ultimate judgment. If the feasibility of the ultimate judgment in chapter 5 was rendered somewhat plausible through the positive categories of creation, in the latter part of Wisdom, the ultimate judgment is based on Israel's history — the exodus.

The hope in an ultimate judgment which the author presented through a series of declarations in the opening part of Wisdom is now shown

---

10:13–14; and finally the Israelites and Moses are contrasted to the plight of their enemies, Pharaoh, and his army. Throughout these contrasts, wisdom is judged to have intervened in order to save and inspire the just.

12. The literary structure of Wisdom 11–19 is a complex interweaving of diptychs with theological reflections. The author's use of diptychs to unfold the plagues and blessings against Pharaoh and for the Israelites is parallel to the four diptychs in Wisdom 3–4. See A. G. Wright, "The Structure of Wisdom 11–19," *CBQ* 27 (1965) 28–34, and Gilbert, "Sagesse de Salomon (ou livre de la Sagesse)," cols. 114–19.

to be based on the great saving event of Israel. Precisely because God has saved the Israelites from Pharaoh's forces in the past, using creation itself, then the postulation of a culminating, ultimate judgment is even more feasible. The author has based the hope of an ultimate judgment on the interpretation of the exodus. It is therefore not surprising to see deliberate parallels between the author's argumentation in the first section of Wisdom and in the final section. The principles regarding creation and salvation enunciated in the opening of Wisdom are now shown to be based on Israel's own concrete history. It is the author's reinterpretation of the exodus events through the lens of creation theology that finally unites creation, the exodus, and salvation into a continuous spectrum.

The two principles which the author explored to link creation to the ultimate judgment in the first section are applied to the reinterpretation of the exodus. a) The cosmos is wholesome because God has created the world and continues to love all things. b) The cosmos itself has been transformed and renewed in order to restore justice for the Israelites and to destroy the chaos of the enemies.

The positive quality of all that God had created is asserted again in order to draw the parallel between creation and the exodus events.

> 11:17   For your all-powerful hand, which created the world out of formless matter . . . (cf. 1:14).
>
> 11:24   For you love all things that exist and detest none of the things that you have made . . . (cf. 1:14).
>
> 11:26   You spare all things, for they are yours, O Lord, you who love the living (cf. 1:13).

The language used to enunciate this interpretive key for the exodus events is similar to the language employed in 1:13–14. Just as the positive relationship between God and the cosmos was established as a basis for the intervention of the cosmos in behalf of the just in Wisdom 1–6, so too is the same relationship presented as a basis for the intervention of the cosmos in behalf of the Israelites during the exodus.

The second principle, whereby the cosmos is understood to intervene in behalf of the Israelites against the enemy, is a unique interpretation of the exodus events by the author of Wisdom.[13] The author recounts

---

13. For the scene of the ultimate judgment in Wisdom 5, the author of Wisdom borrowed the analogy of God being armed with moral virtues from Isaiah. The author's unique

the exodus events with a particular point of view that is formally stated. The very elements of the cosmos that God used to destroy the enemies of the Israelites were the same elements that saved the Israelites (11:5, 18:8).

In recounting the plagues, the author appeals to the same principle used for the ultimate judgment of Wisdom 5. God employs the forces of the cosmos to save the just and to destroy the wicked.

> 16:17 For the universe (ὁ κόσμος) defends the righteous.
>
> 16:24 For creation (κτίσις), serving you who made it, exerts itself to punish the unrighteous, and in kindness relaxes on behalf of those who trust in you.

Finally, this transformation of the elements in behalf of the just and against wickedness during the exodus is presented as a new form of creation.[14]

> 16:25 Therefore, at that time also, changed into all forms, creation (κτίσις) served your all-nourishing bounty, according to the desire of those who had need . . .
>
> 19:6 For the whole creation (κτίσις) in its nature was fashioned anew, complying with your commands, so that your children might be kept unharmed.
>
> 19:18 For the elements changed places with one another, as on a harp the notes vary the nature of the rhythm, while each note remains the same.

In this way, both the ultimate judgment of Wisdom 5 and the recounting of the exodus events are viewed by the author of Wisdom as the

---

adaptation of the analogy was to attribute to the cosmos the function of God's means to bring about justice. Similarly, in the author's adaptation of the plague narratives from Exodus, the author highlights the positive function of the forces and elements in the cosmos to save the just and to punish the enemies.

14. The author's unique interpretation of the plagues as God's "fashioning anew" the elements of the cosmos points to the author's deliberate emphasis of the creation motif in moments of salvation. To understand the author's presentation of the exodus simply as a restoration of order would miss the powerful, underlying motif of creation. It is true that the relationship between creation and order in Genesis 1 is carried over in the Wisdom author's perspective of creation and salvation. Personified wisdom in chapters 9 and 10 is seen to restore humanity continuously onto correct paths. But the deliberate parallelism between creation and salvation in chapter 9, and the description of the exodus event through images of another apocalyptic creation, would suggest that the author is emphasizing the "newness" of the salvation moment that the creation motif carries.

continuation of God's creation through salvation. God uses the cosmos to bring about a re-ordering of creation, particularly the re-establishment of justice. Creation, the Exodus, and Salvation are the continuous spectrum of God's creative activity.

Conclusion

In returning to the two points highlighted at the beginning of this paper from Gibert's study on origins in Scripture, I would like to note some of the Wisdom author's particular nuances of creation theology. The literary cross-referencing that is noticeable between the creation and exodus accounts of Genesis and Exodus is a feature that the Wisdom author turns into an interpretive principle. The cosmos has been created through wisdom and it works for the re-establishment of justice against chaos—especially the ethical chaos of injustice. The exodus events are interpreted by the Wisdom author as God's reestablishment of justice precisely through the workings of creation and the cosmos. The exodus is a new creation that saves.

By the same principle, the author projects this creative, saving activity of God into the future, into an ultimate judgment. The role of the cosmos in the apocalyptic judgment of Wisdom 5 is presented by the author with the same interpretive key as that for the exodus events. The elements of the cosmos do battle against injustice in order to restore justice. Creation and salvation are drawn into direct parallel. The exodus is the prime historical example through which creation and salvation are seen to be joined.

Though the philosophic distinctions inherent in strains of Hellenism may have influenced the Israelite conception of creation to be reduced to its "barest elements," in other directions it has expanded. What is more fully developed in the Book of Wisdom is the extension of creation theology to interpret the entire spectrum of history: creation, exodus, and the ultimate judgment. For the Wisdom author, every human event is ultimately interpreted through the lens of a creational principle. The cosmos, created in the wisdom of God, continues to restore the original justice of creation. Creation is a liberation from chaos, and every saving moment is a form of new creation.

THOMAS H. TOBIN, S.J.

Interpretations of the Creation
of the World
in Philo of Alexandria

Philo of Alexandria (ca. 10 B.C.–A.D. 50) influenced the Christian interpretation of the Bible for centuries. Because of this, analyzing Philo's biblical interpretations can be of immense help in understanding early Christian biblical interpretations. In this article I want to analyze briefly interpretations of the account of the creation of the world in Genesis 1–2 found in Philo's treatise *De Opificio Mundi*.[1] More specifically, I shall concentrate on passages (*Opif.* 15–35, 129–30) which are central to the structure of these interpretations. Although I shall not argue it here, many of the interpretations of the creation of the world found in Philo were probably not of his own making but were part of the exegetical traditions of Hellenistic Judaism on which he drew and, to some extent, reinterpreted.[2]

In order to understand the interpretations of the creation of the world found in Philo, one needs to be reminded that the single most important non-biblical work on which Philo drew was the *Timaeus*, Plato's cosmological dialogue in which Timaeus described the Demiurge's ordering

---

1. I shall make use of the parallel passages from *Legum Allegoriae* 1, and *Quaestiones et Solutiones in Genesin* when appropriate. The translations are basically those found in the *LCL* edition of Philo's works.

2. Philo's own interpretations of the early chapters of Genesis are primarily *allegorical*. None of the interpretations that we shall be looking at are technically speaking allegorical. For a detailed defense of this analysis of Philo, see Thomas H. Tobin, S.J., *The Creation of Man: Philo and the History of Interpretation* (CBQMS 14; Washington: Catholic Biblical Association of America, 1983).

of the world of becoming on the basis of ideas in the intelligible world. Philo's use of Plato's *Timaeus,* however, took place within the context of the early stages of Middle Platonism in which the revival and reinterpretation of the *Timaeus* played a significant role. Before turning to the interpretations of the creation of the world found in Philo, we need first to look at what became of the *Timaeus* after Plato's death and the beginnings of Middle Platonism in the first century B.C.

The Fate of Plato's *Timaeus*
and the Origins of Middle Platonism

The fate of Plato's *Timaeus* after Plato's death in 347 B.C. was an odd combination of interest and neglect. There was a good deal of interest in the *Timaeus* in the generation or so after Plato's death. Both Plato's nephew Speusippus (407–339 B.C.), who succeeded him as head of the Academy, and Xenocrates (396–314 B.C.), who in turn succeeded Speusippus, were deeply influenced by the *Timaeus* even when they reinterpreted or rejected some of its viewpoints. After the death of Xenocrates in 314 B.C. Polemon (ca. 350–267 B.C.) became head of the Academy. Polemon seems not to have been interested in speculation; his interests seem to have been almost entirely ethical in nature.[3] After Polemon's death in 267 B.C., Crantor headed the Academy for a few years and was succeeded by Arcesilaus (316–242 B.C.). With Arcesilaus the Academy took a skeptical turn that was to dominate its thought until sometime in the first-century B.C. Drawing on the early aporetic dialogues of Plato, Arcesilaus held to no doctrines of a positive nature but, following the lead of Socrates, opted for the give-and-take of argument, the result of which led to a withholding of judgment (ἐποχή). In such an atmosphere there was little place for the speculation of the *Timaeus,* and so the *Timaeus* played no role in either the Middle or the New Academy.

This situation changes radically, however, with the beginnings of Middle Platonism (that is the Platonic tradition roughly from 80 B.C. to A.D. 220).[4] Yet the interpretation of Plato's *Timaeus* in Middle Platonism as well as Middle Platonism itself are difficult to understand and that for two general

3. See Diogenes Laërtius 4.18.
4. The best and most thorough treatments of Middle Platonism are J. Dillon, *The Middle Platonists* (Ithaca: Cornell University, 1977) and S. Gersh, *Middle Platonism and Neoplatonism: The Latin Tradition* (2 vols.; Notre Dame: University of Notre Dame, 1986).

reasons. First, what we have of Middle Platonic writings is very fragmentary. We have very few complete Middle Platonic treatises for a philosophical movement that lasted over two hundred years.[5] The rest of our knowledge of Middle Platonic writers and of their interpretations of the *Timaeus* are fragmentary and often culled from later commentaries.

Second, the origins of Middle Platonism are obscure. Various figures (Posidonius of Apamea, Antiochus of Ascalon, Eudorus of Alexandria) have been suggested as its founder(s). While scholars now tend to exclude both Posidonius and Antiochus from the list, the origins of Middle Platonism still remain somewhat of a mystery.[6] Yet evidence does suggest that first-century B.C. Alexandria played an important role in its development. The writings of Philo himself attest to the strength of Middle Platonism in Alexandria by the middle of the first century A.D. Since Philo was unlikely to have been the first to hold such views, one must look to earlier writers for clues to the background of Middle Platonism. Some clues can be found in Alexandria in the first century B.C. The most important figure for these developments was probably Eudorus of Alexandria.

Eudorus of Alexandria (fl. 30 B.C.) lived roughly two generations before Philo. Practically nothing is known of his life. We know little more about his philosophical outlook, but what we know points to several developments that were crucial for the development of Middle Platonism.[7] In

---

5. We have treatises of Plutarch, Alcinous, Albinus, "Timaios of Lokri," and Philo of Alexandria.

6. The influence of Posidonius (c. 135–50 B.C.) on Middle Platonism has been emphasized by W. Jaeger (*Nemesios von Emesa* [Berlin: Weidmann, 1914]) and K. Reinhardt (*Posidonios* [Munich: C. H. Beck, 1921], *Kosmos und Sympathie* [Munich: C. H. Beck, 1926]). However, both L. Edelstein ("The Philosophical System of Posidonius," *AJP* 57 [1936] 286–325) and A. D. Nock ("Posidonius," *Essays on Religion and the Ancient World* [Cambridge: Harvard University, 1972] 853–76) have shown that Posidonius still remained a Stoic and was not of fundamental importance for the development of Middle Platonism. Antiochus of Ascalon's (c. 130–68 B.C.) positions on physics still reflect a Stoic monism. In that sense he cannot be seen as a founder of Middle Platonism. Yet his turn from skepticism and toward the authority of the "ancients" (i.e., Plato, Speusippus, Xenocrates, Polemon, Aristotle, and Theophrastus) was important in establishing the groundwork for Middle Platonism.

7. The two most detailed treatments of Eudorus are H. Dörrie, "Der Platoniker Eudorus von Alexandreia," *Platonica Minora* (Munich: Wilhelm Fink, 1976) 297–307; and Dillon, *The Middle Platonists*, 115–35.

the first place Eudorus seems to have written a commentary on Plato's *Timaeus*.[8] Eudorus was not alone in being interested in the *Timaeus*. Several years earlier Cicero had translated the *Timaeus* into Latin (probably in 45 B.C.). This indicates a fairly wide philosophical interest in reading and interpreting Plato's *Timaeus,* an interest that began perhaps, as early as the latter part of the second century B.C.[9] This is important of course because so much of the physics and theology of Middle Platonism is rooted in the interpretation of the *Timaeus*.

Eudorus also witnesses to the return of the notion of transcendence. Neither the monism of the Stoics nor the agnosticism of the Skeptics (whether inside or outside the New Academy) had room for a transcendent deity. A fragment from Eudorus (Simplicius, *In Phys.* I.5; Diels, 181.7–30) points to just such a transcendence. In this viewpoint, which Eudorus describes as Pythagorean, there is a supreme One which utterly transcends the principles of existing things. This supreme One is called the Supreme God. While Eudorus describes the position as "Pythagorean," the reality may not have been so simple. Neither the old Pythagoreans nor the revived Pythagoreanism of the first century B.C. seems to have held that there was a supreme One above the second One and its opposite, the Unlimited Dyad.[10] Eudorus may well have been more original than he lets on. In any case, the notion of a supreme, transcendent God beyond the basic principles of existing things became a characteristic doctrine of Middle Platonists and deeply affected their interpretations of Plato's *Timaeus*.

Yet the transcendence is of a peculiar sort. The emphasis on the transcendence of the supreme One creates the need for an intermediate realm in which one finds the proximate principles or causes for existing things. In Eudorus this is the realm of the Monad (or second One) and the Unlimited Dyad. These two principles and the opposition between them are the proximate causes of the precarious stability of the world of becoming. The second One, then, becomes an intermediate figure between the supreme One and the Unlimited Dyad. The structure of this

8. Plutarch, *De An. Pro. in Tim.* 16.

9. There is some evidence that both Panaetius and Posidonius had been interested in the *Timaeus*.

10. Alexander Polyhistor *apud* Diogenes Laërtius 8.24–25; Dillon, *The Middle Platonists,* 127.

intermediate realm will be different for each Middle Platonist, but the existence of such a realm will become characteristic of Middle Platonism.

These viewpoints, as we shall see, significantly affected the ways in which Philo interpreted the creation of the world. At this point, however, it is enough to be aware that Philo wrote during the same period and in the same city where Middle Platonism was emerging. Middle Platonism was a crucial part of Philo's intellectual and cultural world.

The Creation of the World in *De Opificio Mundi*

Philo's most extended and detailed interpretation of the creation of the world is found in his treatise *De Opificio Mundi*. This treatise is an interpretation of Gen 1:1–3:24. After a prologue (1–15), the treatise falls basically into three parts: (1) The Creation of the Intelligible and Sense-perceptible Worlds (15–128); (2) The Interpretation of the Creation of Man in Gen 2:7 (129–50); and (3) The Interpretation of the Story of the Fall (151–70a). The treatise then concludes with a section that summarizes the main points Philo wants to make (170b–72). Within *De Opificio Mundi,* however, there are two major and quite distinct interpretations of the creation of the world. The first of these interpretations dominates *Opif.* 15–128; the second dominates *Opif.* 129–50.

1. First Interpretation of the Creation of the World in De Opificio Mundi

The basic structure of the interpretation in the first part of *De Opificio Mundi* (The Creation of the Intelligible and Sense-perceptible Worlds [15–128]) is established at the very beginning of this section, in the interpretation of ἡμέρα μία "day one" (Gen 1:5) in *Opif.* 15–35. Philo emphasizes this structure at both the beginning and the end of the interpretation of "day one" of creation (*Opif.* 15–16, 35):

> Now to each of the days He assigned some of the portions of the whole, not including, however, the first day, which He does not even call "first" (πρώτην), lest it should be reckoned with the others, but naming it "one" (μίαν) He designated it by a name which precisely hits the mark, for He discerned in it and expressed by the title which He gives it the nature and appellation of the unit, or the "one." (*Opif.* 15)

We must recount, as many as we can of the elements embraced in it. To recount them all would be impossible. Its pre-eminent element is the intelligible world (τὸν νοητὸν κόσμον), as is shown in the treatise dealing with the "One." . . . So when He willed to create this visible world (τὸν ὁρατὸν κόσμον) He first fully formed the intelligible world . . . (*Opif.* 16).

When light had come into being, and darkness had moved out of its way and retired, and evening and dawn had been fixed as barriers in the intervals between them, as a necessary consequence a measure of time was forthwith brought about, which its Maker called Day, and not "first" day but "one," an expression due to the uniqueness of the intelligible world (τοῦ νοητοῦ κόσμου), and to its having therefore a natural kinship to the number "One." (*Opif.* 35)

In this interpretation what is created on the first day of creation is the intelligible world (ὁ νοητὸς κόσμος); it is only on the second through the sixth days that the sense-perceptible world (ὁ αἰσθητὸς κόσμος) is created (*Opif.* 36). This intelligible world consists of seven elements: (1) the incorporeal heaven, (2) the invisible earth, the idea of (3) air and (4) the void, the incorporeal essence of (5) water, (6) life-breath (πνεῦμα), and (7) light (*Opif.* 29–32). The exegetical justification for this interpretation is found in the peculiar formulation of Gen 1:5 (ἡμέρα μία instead of ἡμέρα πρώτη). It indicates the unique character of the first day of creation, the natural kinship of the intelligible world to the unit (ἡ μονάς).

Philo also offers explanations of why God went about the creation of the world in this fashion. God, being God, knew beforehand that a beautiful copy (μίμημα καλὸν) would never be produced without a beautiful pattern (δίχα καλοῦ παραδείγματος); and so, when he created this visible world, he first fully formed the intelligible world (*Opif.* 16). Philo then offers the analogy of a king or governor who wants to found a city. The king or governor has an architect draw up a plan for the city beforehand, and so when the city is built it is built according to the incorporeal ideas (τῶν ἀσωμάτων ἰδεῶν) found in this plan (*Opif.* 16–18). The same thing is true of God:

We must suppose that, when He was minded to found the one great city [i.e., the world], He conceived beforehand the models of its parts, and that out of these He constituted and brought to completion an intelligible world, and then with that for a pattern, the sense-perceptible world. (*Opif.* 19)

In this same vein, Philo goes on to explain that the reason for God's creation was God's goodness, that is, he did not grudge (οὐκ ἐφθόνησεν) a share in his own excellent nature to other beings which of themselves had nothing fair or lovely about them but which were capable to undergoing a change for the better, of turning toward the better, toward harmony, toward what is characteristic of the more excellent idea (ἰδέας) (*Opif.* 22).

These interpretations, of course, clearly reflect the basic division of the ordering of the world found in Plato's *Timaeus*.[11] In Plato's *Timaeus* the Demiurge orders the sense-perceptible world on the basis of the ideas in the intelligible world (*Tim.* 27c–29a). In addition, the reasons given for ordering the sense-perceptible world in this way are also very similar. The Demiurge looked to an unchanging model from the intelligible world because only in this way could what was accomplished be good. Because the Demiurge is the best of all causes, the world is the best of all things that have become.

> Now whenever the maker (ὁ δημιουργός) of anything looks to that which is always unchanging and uses a model (παραδείγματι) of that description in fashioning the form and quality of his work, all that he thus accomplishes must be good. If he looks to something that has come to be and uses a generated model, it will not be good. . . . Now if this world is good and its maker is good, clearly he looked to the eternal. . . . Having come to be, then, in this way, the world has been fashioned on the model of that which is comprehensible by rational discourse and understanding and is always in the same state. (*Tim.* 28a–b; 29a)[12]

In addition, Plato's *Timaeus,* in a passage to which Philo explicitly refers in *Opif.* 21, also points to the goodness and generosity of the Demiurge as the reason for the ordering of the world.

> Let us, then, state for what reason becoming and this universe were framed by him who framed them. He was good; and in the good no jealousy (φθόνος) in any matter can ever arise. So, being without jealousy, he desired that all things should come as near as possible to being like

11. For a very fine and detailed study of the relationship of Philo's interpretations to Plato's *Timaeus,* see D. T. Runia, *Philo of Alexandria and the* Timaeus *of Plato* (Philosophia Antiqua 44; Leiden: Brill, 1986).

12. The translations of Plato's *Timaeus* are from F. M. Cornford, *Plato's Cosmology* (New York: Humanities, 1937).

himself. That this is the supremely valid principle of becoming and of the order of the world, we shall most surely be right to accept from men of understanding. Desiring, then, that all things should be good and, so far as might be, nothing imperfect, the god took over all that is visible—not at rest, but in discordant and unordered motion—and brought it from disorder into order, since he judged that order was in every way the better. (*Tim.* 29d–30a)

The way in which Philo structures his interpretation of the creation of the world, then, is clearly derived from Plato's *Timaeus.*

Yet Philo's interpretation reflects not simply Plato's *Timaeus* but also the way in which the *Timaeus* came to be interpreted in the early stages of Middle Platonism. This emerges most clearly in Philo's use of the *logos.*

Should someone desire to use words more simply, he would say that the intelligible world is nothing else than the Word of God when He was already engaged in the act of creation (θεοῦ λόγον ἤδη κοσμο- ποιοῦντος). For (to revert to our illustration) the intelligible city is nothing else than the reasoning faculty (λογισμός) of the architect in the act of planning to found the city. It is Moses who lays down this, not I. Witness his express acknowledgement in the sequel, when setting on record the creation of man, that he was modelled after the image of God (Gen 1:27). Now if the part is an image of an image, it is manifest that the whole is so too, and if the whole creation, this entire sense-perceptible world (seeing that it is greater than any human image) is a copy of the Divine image (μίμημα θείας εἰκόνος), it is manifest that the archetypal seal also, which we aver to be the intelligible world, would be the very Word of God (ὁ θεοῦ λόγος). (*Opif.* 24–25)

In this interpretation the intelligible world of Gen 1:1–5 is identified with the λόγος of God as God is engaged in creation. Philo first illustrates this by referring back to his comparison of God's act of creating to the architect's process of reasoning by which he first forms a plan (the intelligible city) before he actually goes about building the city (*Opif.* 17–20). In *Opif.* 20, the conclusion of the passage to which he refers, Philo makes a similar claim, that the "world that consisted of ideas (ὁ ἐκ τῶν ἰδεῶν κόσμος) would have no other location than the divine Word (τὸν θεῖον λόγον), which is that which orders these things."

He then goes on to offer an exegetical justification for this viewpoint. He points out that the text of Gen 1:27 says that man was formed after the image of God (κατ' εἰκόνα θεοῦ). The κατά in the phrase κατ' εἰκόνα θεοῦ is taken to mean not "*as* an image" but "*according to* or *after* an image." The image according to which man is created is obviously something other than man himself. But it is also something other than God since the image of God is not God himself but his *image*. The image must be a *tertium quid,* and for Philo that *tertium quid* is God's *logos.*[13] By use of the argument *a minore ad maius,* Philo then argues that if the part (i.e., man) is an image of an image, so too must the whole (i.e., the whole sense-perceptible world) be an image of an image, that is, an image of the *logos,* the Word of God.

The figure of the *logos* played a significant role in Philo's biblical interpretations. Philo depicted the *logos* in a variety of ways, and the figure had a number of different functions. One of those functions, as in *Opif.* 24–25, was cosmological. The *logos* was the image of God, the highest of all beings who were intellectually perceived, the one closest to God, the only truly existent (*Fug.* 101). This image, the *logos,* also served as the paradigm or model for the ordering of the rest of the universe (*Som.* 2.45). The *logos* was an image in a twofold way, a reflection of the truly existent God above and a model on the basis of which the rest of the universe below was ordered. The *logos* was the archetypal idea in which all of the other ideas were contained (*Opif.* 24–25).

But the *logos* was not simply the image or paradigm according to which the universe was ordered, it was also the instrument (ὄργανον) through which the universe was ordered (*Cher.* 127; *Spec.*1.81). The *logos* was both the power through which the universe was originally ordered and the power by which the universe continued to be ordered. Philo called these two aspects of the *logos* the "Creative Power" and the "Ruling Power," and he connected the first with the name Elohim (God) and the second with Lord (κύριος), the Greek word used (or at least spoken) for Yahweh in the LXX (*Mos.* 2.99–100). Other terms used by Philo to refer to the *logos* are the "First-Begotten Son of the Uncreated Father" (*Conf.* 146; *Som.* 1.215), the "Chief of the Angels" (*Her.* 205), the "High Priest of the Cosmos" (*Fug.* 108), and the "Man of God" (*Conf.* 41, 63, 146). What was common to all of these designations of the *logos* was the intermediate role that the *logos* played between the transcendent God and the rest of the universe.

13. This interpretation is also found in *Leg.* 3.95–96, *Her.* 230–32, *Spec.* 1.80–81; 3.83, 207, and *QG* 2.62.

Because the *logos* functions in such a complex way in Philo's Biblical interpretations, it is often difficult to understand precisely what he meant in those interpretations. Is the *logos* only a metaphor for God's power, a hypostatization of some aspect of God, or a reality distinct from if not independent of God? Is the *logos* personal or impersonal? The answers to these questions can never be altogether clear, but one can gain a basic sense of what Philo meant. Philo thought that God in his essence could not be implicated in the material universe. At the same time, the relative order of the material universe had to derive at least indirectly from God. For Philo the *logos* served as the intermediate metaphysical reality through which the universe was originally ordered and by which it continued to be sustained in an orderly state. On the one hand, then, the *logos* was not simply a metaphor. It was meant to serve as a real explanation, one which safeguarded both the transcendence of God and the relative order of the universe. On the other hand, it was not a description of a being other than God. It was a *real* aspect of the divine reality through which God was related, although indirectly, to the universe.[14] In much the same way, the *logos* cannot aptly be characterized as either personal or impersonal. It was rather the source of the intelligibility of the universe and so was itself intelligent in a way that transcended the universe and, in that sense, also went beyond the categories of either personal or impersonal.

Philo's use of the *logos* as an intermediate figure places him within the larger context of the development of Middle Platonism in which such an intermediate figure was characteristic. As was mentioned above, a recurrent pattern in most Middle Platonists is one which distinguishes in some fashion between an utterly transcendent God and an intermediate reality by which or through which the cosmos is actually ordered.[15] In this way the Demiurge of Plato's *Timaeus* is divided in two. This division creates the triadic pattern which is characteristic of most Middle Platonists: a transcendent primal god, an intermediate reality through which the cosmos is ordered, and matter which is what is given order. This viewpoint, of course, is reflected in Philo's interpretations of the creation of the world. What distinguishes Philo's use of the intermediate figure (the

14. See Runia, *Philo of Alexandria and the* Timaeus *of Plato*, 446–51.

15. For examples of such intermediate figures, see "Timaios of Lokri," *De natura mundi et animae* 1–7 (first century A.D.); Alcinous (Albinus), *Didaskalikos* X, 164.6–166.13 (second century A.D.); and Numenius, Frgs. 11, 15, 16, 19) (second century A.D.).

logos) from other Middle Platonists (e.g., Alcinous and Numenius) is that Philo is quite careful not to make the *logos* a reality *independent* of God and so not to compromise Jewish monotheism.[16]

Philo is also distinguished from most Middle Platonists by his use of the term to identify this intermediate reality.[17] The concept of *logos*, of course, had long been central to Stoicism. For the Stoics, *logos*, God, and nature were in reality one.[18] *Logos* was the rational element that pervades and controls all of the universe.[19] *Logos* was the active element (τὸ ποιοῦν) of reality while matter without quality was the passive element (τὸ πάσχον).[20] The *logos* which permeated the universe was present in nature through seminal reasons (λόγοι σπερματικοί) which served as the powers of order and growth in individual entities.[21] For the Stoics, however, all of these elements were ultimately material.[22]

Philo and the Middle Platonists, in contrast to the Stoics and in keeping with their Platonic orientation, emphasized the primary reality of the immaterial, intelligible realm. Yet Philo and a few Middle Platonists seem to have taken over the Stoic term *logos;* but they also significantly reinterpreted it as part of the immaterial, intelligible realm. Interestingly enough and for reasons which are not entirely clear, this reinterpretation of the Stoic *logos* as an intermediate reality in the intelligible realm seems to have taken place primarily in Alexandria.[23] Eudorus of Alexandria may have referred to the demiurgic combination of the Monad,

---

16. This is emphasized by Runia, *Philo of Alexandria and the* Timaeus *of Plato*, 438–51.

17. See Dillon, *The Middle Platonists*, 46.

18. Diogenes Laërtius 7.135; Plutarch, *De Stoic. repugn.* 34, 1050A.

19. J. von Arnim, ed., *Stoicorum Veterum Fragmenta* (4 vols.; Stuttgart: Teubner, 1968) 1. 87.

20. Diogenes Laërtius 7.134.

21. *Stoicorum Veterum Fragmenta* 2. 1027.

22. *Logos* was identified by Zeno of Citium (335–263 B.C.), the founder of Stoicism, with fire and by Stoics from Chrysippus (ca. 280–207 B.C.) on with a blend of fire and air, which they referred to as breath or spirit (πνεῦμα). The passive element was identified with earth and water. See A. A. Long, *Hellenistic Philosophy* (2d ed.; London: Duckworth, 1986) 155.

23. The connection of the *logos* as an intermediate figure with Alexandria cannot be pressed too far. Both John 1:1–18 (the Prologue of John) and what may be first-century A.D. sections of the *Trimorphic Protennoia* (46.5–6; 47.5–22; 49.22–29, 50.9–12, 18–20) cannot be traced to any particular place, although Alexandria cannot be excluded. For the *Trimorphic Protennoia*, see J. D. Turner, "Trimorphic Protennoia," *The Nag Hammadi Library* (ed. J. M. Robinson; 3d ed.; San Francisco: Harper & Row, 1988) 511–13.

which represented form, and the Dyad, which represented matter, as the thought (*logos*) of the essentially transcendent God, the First or Supreme One.[24] The *logos* as an intermediary figure appears in the *Poimandres* 10–11, a first or second century A.D. treatise from Egypt which, although not Jewish, draws on both Plato's *Timaeus* and the early chapters of Genesis.[25] The most important passage in which the *logos* appears as an intermediate figure is in Plutarch (c. 50–120 A.D.) (*De Is. et Os.* 53–54, 372E–373C). The *logos*, which was identified with the Egyptian God Osiris, was that which ordered and made manifest the material world and at the same time served as the intelligible paradigm for that world. Both the myths about Osiris and Plutarch's interpretations of the myths are probably to be located in first-century A.D. Alexandria.[26] In any case, this interpretation of the creation of the world in Philo clearly reflects not only the influence of Plato's *Timaeus* but also the influence of the early stages of Alexandrian Middle Platonism.

2. Second Interpretation of the Creation of the World

There is, however, an alternate interpretation of the division of the creation of the intelligible world and the creation of the sense-perceptible world. This interpretation dominates *Opif.* 129–50. In this interpretation everything created in Gen 1:1–2:3 is part of the intelligible world. It is only in Gen 2:6 that the creation of the sense-perceptible world begins. This interpretation is found in *Opif.* 129–30:

> In his concluding summary of the story of creation he says: "This is the book of the genesis of heaven and earth, when they came into being, at the time when (ἡ ἡμέρα) God made the heaven and the earth and every herb in the field before it appeared (πρὸ τοῦ γενέσθαι) upon the earth, and all grass of the field before it sprang up (πρὸ τοῦ ἀνατεῖλαι)" (Gen 2:4–5 LXX). Is he not manifestly describing the incorporeal and intelligible ideas (τὰς ἀσωμάτους καὶ νοητὰς ἰδέας), which served as seals of

---

24. Dillon, *The Middle Platonists,* 128.

25. For introductions to the *Poimandres* and the Hermetic Corpus see A. D. Nock and A.-J. Festugière, *Corpus Hermeticum* (Paris: Société d'Édition "Les Belles Lettres," 1972) I. 1–28 and B. Layton, *The Gnostic Scriptures* (Garden City, NY: Doubleday, 1987) 447–51.

26. See J. Gwyn Griffiths, *Plutarch's De Iside et Osiride* (Cardiff: University of Wales, 1970) 41–48; Tobin, *The Creation of Man,* 73–76.

the finished sense-perceptible objects? For before the earth put forth its young green shoots, young verdure was present, he tells us, in the nature of things, and before grass sprang up in the field, there was in existence an invisible grass.

We must suppose that in the case of all other objects also, on which the sense pronounces judgment, the elder forms and measures (τὰ πρεσβύτερα εἴδη καὶ μέτρα), to which all things that come into being owe shape and size, subsisted before them; for even if he has not dealt with everything together (ἀθρόα) according to genus (κατὰ γένος),[27] aiming as he does at brevity in a high degree, nevertheless what he does say gives us a few indications of universal Nature, which brings forth no finished product in the world of sense without using an incorporeal pattern (ἄνευ ἀσωμάτου παραδείγματος).

In this interpretation, Gen 2:4–5 is seen as a summary of everything that has gone before, that is, Gen 1:1–2:3. The exegetical justification for the interpretation that Gen 2:4–5 indicates that the creation described in Gen 1:1–2:3 was that of the intelligible world rests on the peculiar wording of Gen 2:4–5. The interpretation is based on the observation that, according to Gen 2:4–5 (LXX), Gen 1:1–2:3 describe the creation of the heaven and the earth and every herb "before it appeared (πρὸ τοῦ γενέσθαι) on the earth" and all the grass "before it sprang up" (πρὸ τοῦ ἀνατεῖλαι). This means that what was described in Gen 1:1–2:3 was the creation of the intelligible world.

At first it may seem as if the phrase "in the *day* in which" (ἧ ἡμέρᾳ) (Gen 2:4) means that the line of demarcation between the creation of the intelligible world and the creation of the sense-perceptible world in *Opif.* 129–30 is still between "day one" and the other five days, that is that the intelligible paradigms of heaven, earth, herbs, and grass were all created on "day *one.*" Yet the interpretation of these two verses in *Opif.* 129–30 seems to bypass the phrase "in the day in which," since it is not mentioned at all in the interpretation of Gen 2:4–5: The phrase is taken to mean nothing more precise than "at the time when." This becomes clear when one analyzes the phrases "according to genus" (κατὰ γένος)

27. All of the manuscripts except M read κατὰ μέρος rather than κατὰ γένος. To read κατὰ μέρος, however, one must, as Cohn did, emend the text by inserting ‹ἀλλ'› between μέρος and ἀθρόα in order to establish the contrast between μέρος and ἀθρόα. If, however, one reads κατὰ γένος with manuscript M (which with manuscript V is the best) one need make no emendation. As we shall see, this fits the context of *Op.* 129–30 better.

and the "elder forms" (τὰ πρεσβύτερα εἴδη) in *Opif.* 130. The use of these phrases is based on the distinction of genus (γένος) as identical with "idea" or "intelligible paradigm" and form (εἴδος) as identical with "form-in-matter."[28] The term *"elder* forms" then is another way of referring to the "ideas" or "genera" since the forms are copies of pre-existent ideas which are therefore "elder" forms (*Opif.* 130). In this way the terms "incorporeal and intelligible ideas" (*Opif.* 129), the "elder forms and measures" (*Opif.* 130), and "genus" (*Opif.* 130) are synonymous.

In addition, when Philo admits that Moses has not dealt with everything "according to genus," he is referring back to those places in the creation account of Genesis 1 where Moses does recount the creation of plants on the third day (Gen 1:11), fish and birds on the fifth day (Gen 1:21), and land animals on the sixth day (Gen 1:24–25), all "according to genus." For Philo this means that all of these creations are part of the intelligible world. For the sake of brevity, however, Moses has not mentioned in the summary of Gen 2:4–5, the creation of *each* thing "according to genus." Nevertheless, Philo claims, all sense-perceptible objects must have intelligible paradigms which existed before them (*Opif.* 130).

Not only the herbs and the grass mentioned in Gen 2:4–5, then, but also everything else, including the sun, moon, stars, and the man created in Gen 1:27 must be part of the intelligible world of paradigms. The line of demarcation between the creation of the intelligible world and the creation of the sense-perceptible world is no longer at Gen 1:5 (between "day one" and the other days) but at Gen 2:5 (roughly between the Priestly and the Yahwist accounts of creation).

The interpretation in *Opif.* 129–30 is not an isolated interpretation but is of a piece with interpretations found in *Leg.* 1.19–27; 2.11b, 13 and *QG* 1.2, 19 in which all of the creation account in Gen 1:1–2:3 again refers to the creation of the intelligible world, that is, "according to genus."

As the interpretation which placed the division between "day one" and the other five days had a place for the *logos,* so too this interpretation also finds a role for the *logos.* This interpretation is found in *Leg.* 1.19:

---

28. This kind is distinction between γένος and εἴδος is a Middle Platonic reworking of Aristotelian modes of classification. In various forms, this distinction was fairly common in Middle Platonism. See Arius Didymus *apud* Eusebius, *Praep. Evang.* 11.23; Seneca, *Ep.* 58.16, 18–21; Alcinous (Albinus), *Didaskalikos* X, 165.37–166.6; and Tobin, *The Creation of Man,* 114–19.

> This book (ἡ βίβλος) is that of the origin of heaven and earth, when it come into being (Gen 2:4). (That is to say): This perfect Reason (λόγος), moving in accord with the number seven, is the primal origin both of mind ordering itself after the original patterns, and of sense-perception in the domain of mind (if the expression is permissible) ordering itself after those originals. "Book" (βιβλίον) is Moses' name for the Reason of God (τὸν τοῦ θεοῦ λόγον), in which have been inscribed and engraved the formation of all else.

In this interpretation, the *logos* of God is the place where all that is described in Gen 1:1–2:3 occurs. This means that all that is described in Gen 1:2–2:3 takes place in the intelligible world, which is identified as the *logos* of God. Once again, the *logos* plays an intermediate role in the creation of the world. This interpretation is then spelled out in more detail in *Leg.* 1.21–25 in a way which is similar to but not identical with the interpretation found in *Opif.* 129–30.

3. Relationship of These Interpretations to the Creation of Man

Given the complexity of these interpretations, neither of them represents odd or eccentric interpretations. Both represent quite consistent and well thought-out analyses of the biblical text. This becomes clearer when one realizes that each of these two interpretations of the creation of the world has a parallel interpretation of the creation of man.

There are a number of passages in Philo in which the creation of man in Gen 1:26–27 and Gen 2:7 is interpreted in a way that is consistent with the division of the creation of the intelligible world from the creation of the sense-perceptible world at Gen 1:5 (*Opif.* 139, 145–46, *Spec.* 1.171, *Her.* 55–57, *Det.* 80–90, *Plant.* 14–27, *Mut.* 223, *Virt.* 103–5). There is no distinction made between the two creation accounts; the man created in Gen 1:27 and the man created in Gen 2:7 are identical. In addition, there is no explicit indication in these interpretations that the creation of man is on the basis of some heavenly paradigm or idea of "man."

There are also a number of passages in which the creation of man is described in a way that is consistent with the division of the creation of the intelligible world from the creation of the sense-perceptible world at Gen 2:5 (*Opif.* 134–35, *Leg.* 1.31–32, *QG* 1.4, 8a, 2.56). In the latter case, there are two men who are created, one in the intelligible world

(Gen 1:27) and the other in the sense-perceptible world (Gen 2:7). The clearest example of this second interpretation of the creation of man is found in *Opif.* 134–35:

> After this he says that "God formed man by taking clay from the earth, and breathed into his face the breath of life" (Gen 2:7). By this also he shows very clearly that there is a vast difference between the man thus formed and the man that came into existence earlier after the image of God (Gen 1:27); for the man so formed is an object of sense perception, partaking already of such or such quality, consisting of body and soul, man or woman, by nature mortal; while he that was after the image was an idea, or genus, or seal, intelligible, incorporeal, neither male nor female, by nature incorruptible.
>
> It says, however, that the formation of the individual man, the object of sense, is a composite one made up of earthly substance and of divine spirit; for it says that the body was made through the Artificer taking clay and molding out of it a human form, but that the soul was originated from nothing created whatever, but from the Father and Ruler of all; for that which He breathed in was nothing else than a divine spirit that migrated hither from that blissful and happy existence for the benefit of our race, to the end that, even if it is mortal in respect of its visible part, it may in respect of the part that is invisible be rendered immortal. Hence it may with propriety be said that man is the borderland between mortal and immortal nature, partaking of each so far as is needful, and that he was created at once mortal and immortal, mortal in respect of the body, but in respect of the mind immortal.

The exegetical justification for this interpretation becomes clearer when one places the characteristics of the two men aside by side.

A. The man made according to the image (Gen 1:27)	B. The molded man (Gen 2:7)
1. intelligible	1. sense perceptible
2. idea, type, seal	2. partaking of qualities
3. incorporeal	3. *made of body and soul*
4. *neither male nor female*	4. male or female
5. by nature incorruptible	5. by nature mortal

When one looks at this table, two of the characteristics are obviously the result of interpretations of the two verses from Genesis (Gen 1:27 and Gen 2:7). Those characteristics are: (1) neither male nor female (Gen 1:27); and (2) made of body and soul. The text of Gen 1:27 says that

God made man "male *and* female" (ἄρσεν καὶ θῆλυ). This is taken to mean not that the first man was an androgyne but that he was *neither* male *nor* female and so prior to any sexual differentiation. This characteristic contrasts with what is said about the man created in Gen 2:7. In Gen 2:7 there is no indication that the man is "male and female." On the contrary, the creation of the man in Gen 2:7 is followed by the creation of woman (Gen 2:21–22), and so the man created in Gen 2:7 is sexually differentiated, that is, he is male.

The detail that is singled out in Gen 2:7 is the fact that "God formed man by taking clay from the *earth,* and breathed into his face the *breath of life.*" This is taken to mean that the man created in Gen 2:7 was composed of *body* (earth) and *soul* (breath of life), that is, he was a composite being. By contrast, there is no indication in the text of Gen 1:27 that the man created there was a being composed of body and soul.

Expanding on these two details in the text, the interpretation then goes on to maintain that the man created in Gen 1:27, because simple and prior to any sexual distinction, must have belonged to the intelligible realm, to the realm of idea, genus, or seal. Conversely the man created in Gen 2:7 must belong to the sense-perceptible realm.

Levels of Interpretation

Given the fact that both of these interpretations of the creation of the world (and of man) are well developed interpretations, both of which draw on Plato's *Timaeus* and Middle Platonism, one needs to ask the question about the relationship between these two interpretations. The most plausible explanation is that these two interpretations represent two distinct levels of interpretation in which the second layer (i.e., the division between the intelligible world and the sense-perceptible world at Gen 2:5) is somewhat later and dependent on the first layer of interpretation (i.e., the division between the two worlds at Gen 1:5).

Perhaps the best indicator of the relationship between these two layers of interpretation is provided by the two interpretations of the story of the creation of man. As I have argued elsewhere, an analysis of the contents and the language of the two interpretations of the creation of man indicate that the interpretation which distinguishes between the creation of a heavenly, intelligible "man" in Gen 1:27 from an earthly, sense-perceptible man in Gen 2:7 takes up the concepts and language of the interpretations in which Gen 1:27 and 2:7 were seen as the creation of a single man (that is, which did not distinguish between the two accounts).[29] This shows that the interpretation that involves the creation of a single man is the earlier level of interpretation on which the later level of interpretation, that is, the double creation of man, depends. Because these two interpretations of the creation of man are intimately interwoven with the two interpretations of the creation of the world, the same relationship holds between these two levels of interpretation. The interpretation which places the division between the creation of the intelligible world and the creation of the sense-perceptible world at Gen 1:5 is the prior interpretation on which depends the interpretation in which the division between the creation of the two worlds is placed at Gen 2:5.

The reason for the development of this second level of interpretation is connected with parallel developments in the Middle Platonic philosophical tradition. When Plato described the creation of man in *Tim.* 40d–47e, he did not mention the use of a paradigm from the intelligible world in that creation.[30] Yet, at least by the latter part of the first century B.C., the notion of a model or paradigm for man had probably become a philosophical commonplace. In a fragment from the first-century B.C. Alexandrian philosopher Arius Didymus' *On the Doctrines of Plato,* we find the following explanation of the Platonic ideas.

> He (Plato) says that the ideas (ἰδέας) are certain patterns (τινὰ παρα-δείγματα) arranged class by class (κατὰ γένος) of the things which are by nature sense-perceptible (τῶν αἰσθητῶν), and that these are the sources of the different sciences and definitions. For *besides all individual men there is a certain conception of man;* and besides all horses, of a horse; and generally besides the animals, a conception of an animal uncreated and imperishable (ἀγένητον καὶ ἄφθαρτον).
>
> And in the same way as many impressions are made of one seal, and many images of one man, so from each single idea of the objects of sense a multitude of individual natures are formed, *from the idea of man all men,* and in like manner in the case of all other things in nature. Also the idea is an eternal essence (ἀΐδιον οὐσίαν), cause, and principle, making each thing to be of a character such as its own. (Eusebius, *Praep. Evang.* 11,23).

29. Tobin, *The Creation of Man,* 56–134.

30. Aristotle (*Metaphy.* 1.9–15, 991[ab]) indicates that Plato had an "idea" of man, but that notion is not found clearly in the Platonic texts themselves. The "idea" of man as a standard example became popular in the Platonic tradition only later.

Arius Didymus is giving what must have been an interpretation of the Platonic ideas fairly common in the latter half of the first century B.C. Prominent among these ideas is the idea or paradigm of man, a paradigm that is uncreated and imperishable and that serves as a seal for the creation of particular men who are then images of that one seal.[31]

This same viewpoint is found in the interpretations of the double creation of man in *Opif.* 134–35 and *Leg.* 1.31–32. The popularity of the Middle Platonic notion of the idea or paradigm of "man" probably led Jewish interpreters to see in the two accounts of the creation of man in Gen 1:27 and 2:7 a similar distinction between the creation of the ideal, intelligible man in Gen 1:27 and the creation of the earthly, sense-perceptible man in Gen 2:7.

This interpretation, however, also created a certain inconsistency between this interpretation of the double creation of man and the interpretation of the creation of the world which placed the division between the intelligible world and the sense-perceptible world at Gen 1:5. The creation of the intelligible man in Gen 1:27 now took place at a point which should have been part of the account of the creation of the *sense-perceptible* world. At least in significant part, this then led to the rearrangement of the point of division between the creations of the two different worlds. Based on the peculiar wording of Gen 2:4–5, that new division was now placed at Gen 2:5, roughly at the division between the Priestly and the Yahwist accounts of creation.

Conclusions

Several tentative conclusions can be drawn from this analysis of the interpretations of the creation of the world found in Philo. The first is that Philo was part of a larger tradition of Hellenistic Jewish biblical interpretation and that this larger tradition played a significant role in Philo's interpretations. While we did not go into the relationship of Philo to this larger tradition in any detail, it is clear from the texts we did analyze that the biblical text was not interpreted simply by itself. Rather it was interpreted within the context of a larger exegetical tradition. The development of the second layer of the interpretation of the creation of the world, which placed the division between the intelligible and the sense-perceptible

31. See also Seneca, *Ep.* 58, 18–19.

worlds at Gen 2:5, was due at least in part to the necessity of reinter-
preting the previous level of interpretation (that placed the division at
Gen 1:5) that was caused by the development of the interpretation of Gen
1:27 and Gen 2:7 as a double creation of man.

A second conclusion is that these interpretations were not cavalier but
were based on a close reading of the biblical text. As we analyzed them,
we found that there was an exegetical justification given for each of the
interpretations. The justification was based on noting a particular element
in the biblical text, often enough an element that seemed odd. That odd
element then served as the basis for the interpretation that followed. A
crucial phrase in a verse was interpreted in such a way that it pointed
the interpreter toward a certain set of philosophical concepts. Once that
connection, that bridge, had been established, the philosophical concepts
could then be used to interpret the whole passage. These exegetical
justifications were of various sorts: an argument from a particular word
(*Opif.* 15, 24, 35, 129–30, 134–35); an argument from appropriateness (*Opif.*
35); an argument based on an analogy (*Opif.* 17–20); an argument *a
minore ad maius* (*Opif.* 24–25). While modern biblical scholars would
quite rightly find many of the exegetical arguments in Philo specious,
I want to emphasize that the real reason for this evaluation is that Philo's
presuppositions about the nature of the biblical text were different from
the more "historically" oriented presuppositions of modern scholars, and
not that he did not give the biblical text a "close reading." For Philo the
biblical text was a seamless robe in which every strand counted and had
its proper place, where every detail, however odd, had its significance
for the interpretation of the biblical text as a whole.

A third and final conclusion has to do with the relationship of these
interpretations to the larger world of Greek philosophical thought,
specifically emerging Middle Platonism. These interpretations have been
clearly influenced by the thought of Plato's *Timaeus* and its reinterpretation in Middle Platonism. One could, and scholars probably will, argue
forever about whether or not these interpretations represent a betrayal
of Judaism, the "acute (and illegitimate) Hellenization" of Judaism. But
in these arguments it is important to keep in mind how Philo and probably other interpreters in that tradition viewed what they were about.
At the beginning of *De Opificio Mundi* Philo tells his readers his overall
view of the significance of Moses' account of the creation of the world:

His (Moses') exordium, as I have said, is one that excites our admiration in the highest degree. It consists of an account of the creation of the world, implying that the world is in harmony with the Law, and the Law with the world (καὶ τοῦ κόσμου τῷ νόμῳ καὶ τοῦ νόμου τῷ κόσμῳ συνᾴδοντος), and that the man who observes the Law is constituted a loyal citizen of the world, regulating his doings by the purpose of Nature (πρὸς τὸ βούλημα τῆς φύσεως), in accordance with which the entire world itself also is administered. (*Opif.* 3)

Philo's view of Moses' account of the creation of the world claims that it is ultimately in harmony with "nature" and, of course, in harmony with the God who is the author of that "nature." It would not be surprising then that such an account would also be reflected in the best Greek philosophical thought, i.e., in Plato's *Timaeus* (*Opif.* 21). But for Philo it is always the Mosaic Law which best understood "nature" and its laws. He speaks in a similar way at the end of the treatise:

He that has begun by learning these things with his understanding rather than with his hearing, and has stamped on his soul impressions of truths so marvelous and priceless, both that (1) God is and is from eternity, and that (2) He that really is is One and that (3) He has made the world and (4) has made it one world, unique as he Himself is unique, and that (5) He ever exercises forethought for His creation, will lead a life of bliss and blessedness, because he has a character molded by the truths that piety and holiness enforce. (*Opif.* 172)

These five elements that Philo sees as the central elements in Moses' interpretation of the creation of the world are certainly indebted in significant ways to Plato's *Timaeus* both for their content and for their formulation. Yet at the same time, it would be difficult to claim that any of them represent views that are not in harmony with the biblical account of creation.

JOAN E. COOK, S.C.

Creation in 4 Ezra:
The Biblical Theme
in Support of Theodicy

The creation accounts in 4 Ezra invite reflection on three interactive sets of questions of interest to the theology of the Hebrew Bible/Old Testament. Proceeding from the general to the particular, the first set concerns the theological task: Who is God? Who/what is creation? What is the relationship between them? The second relates to the task of biblical interpretation: How does the book remain faithful to the Torah? How does it differ? The third recognizes a significant characteristic of biblical creation accounts: What larger concern do these creation stories serve? In this study I will first comment on these sets of questions. Then I will examine three passages in 4 Ezra that discuss creation at some length: 6:1–6, 38–59 and 16:53–63, which appears in the appendix.[1] I will then

1. I use the term 4 Ezra to designate chaps. 3–14, as opposed to 2 Esdras, which entitles the book in its canonical form, chaps. 1–16. The lack of original or early manuscripts of the book prevents certainty regarding the language, date, provenance, and unity of the book. However, certain internal evidence offers clues. 3:1 and chaps. 11–12 suggest ca. 100 C.E. as the date of composition of chaps. 3–14. The original language and textual history of the book are likewise uncertain, but the Hebraisms in the text lead to general agreement that Hebrew is the original language from which the work was translated into Greek. All the extant versions (Arabic, Ethiopic, Georgian, Latin, Slavonic and Syriac), the earliest of which dates to the ninth century, are thought to have come from the Greek. The place of composition is even more problematic, but is thought to be Palestine. Chaps. 1–2 (5 Ezra, or the introduction) and 15–16 (6 Ezra, or the appendix) are understood to be later additions because they are not included in the Eastern versions, and because they differ ideologically from chaps. 3–14. Metzger ascribes Christian authorship to the sections, which he dates between 250 and 300 C.E., but he does not offer a discussion of

reflect on the insights these passages offer into the three sets of questions and their usefulness for the project of Hebrew Bible/Old Testament Theology.

First, regarding the theological task, the questions appear by their very simplicity to belabor the obvious. But pragmatically, the obvious is frequently most difficult to see. And theoretically, the simplicity of the questions lies in their foundational significance rather than in facile answers.

The second set of questions takes as its point of departure the normative place of the Torah within the Bible, and provides a measuring rod against which to observe how 4 Ezra continues and how it adapts the notions in the Genesis accounts—a testimonial to the vitality and universality of the theme of creation.

The third group of questions recognizes that the biblical creation accounts illustrate other themes beyond the process or product of creation. In fact, this set of questions introduces a caveat implicit in the present study; that is, while the creation theme plays a significant part in the development of 4 Ezra's ideas throughout the book, it is not the primary point of the work. My project proposes not to clarify the book's concern with questions of theodicy, but rather to demonstrate the use of the creation theme to illustrate that point.

Typical of Jewish apocalyptic literature toward the end of the first century C.E., 4 Ezra describes seven visions which Ezra the seer receives from the Lord and/or the divine messenger Uriel. The first two passages in this study are contained in these visions. The third appears in the appendix (chapters 15–16).

In the first three visions Ezra grapples explicitly and painfully with the question that vexed Jews toward the end of the first century C.E.: Why the Roman destruction of Jerusalem?[2] Ezra's efforts not only to find

---

the matter. Charlesworth and Myers clarify the variety of titles for the various Ezra materials. For detailed discussions of these vexing questions, see B. M. Metzger, "The Fourth Book of Ezra," *The Old Testament Pseudepigrapha* (ed. J. H. Charlesworth; 2 vols.; Garden City, NY: Doubleday, 1983) 1. 516, 518–20; J. M. Myers, *I & II Esdras* (AB 42; Garden City, NY: Doubleday, 1974) 107–8, 112–19, 129; and M. E. Stone, *Fourth Ezra: A Commentary on the Book of Fourth Ezra* (Hermeneia; Minneapolis: Fortress, 1990) 1–11, 56–57.

2. In the fourth through seventh visions Ezra confronts larger questions about life after death, reward and punishment in the next life for how we have lived this life, and whether humans are inherently good or evil.

answers to the question but also to come to terms with his own situation show movement from vision to vision as well as within each vision. Michael Stone's delineation of the structure of chapters 3–14 illustrates this dynamic.[3]

The first passage, 6:1–6, is part of the dialogical prediction in Vision 2, concerning the end of the age. The Lord speaks in response to Ezra's request to learn the agent of the impending judgment. The divine response indicates that God will cause the end time, and emphasizes the point by cataloging the divine causality of the cosmos.

The description of divine creation resembles Prov 8:22–29 and Psalm 90 in style and content. The scope of divine creative activity extends beyond the cosmological to include meteorological phenomena (vv 1–2), paradise (v 2), flowers (v 3), angels (v 4), Zion (v 4), human imagination and destiny (v 5).[4] The specific reference to the footstool of Zion alludes to the special place of the Jews in creation. This motif will become explicit in the second passage.

The catalog of creatures takes the form of a series of clauses introduced by "and before"[5] to highlight two particular aspects of the creator: divine causality and purposefulness. The three-fold declaration in v 6 encompasses all of time in three distinct stages: the planning stage, creation itself, and the end time. It emphasizes that the one creator is the sole agent in all three stages, repeating "through me and not through another" in two of the three assertions.[6] By declaring, "I planned these things" the divine speaker emphasizes the purposefulness of creation: the creator mapped out each aspect of creation, including not only the

3. Stone, *Ezra,* 51.

4. Lists of things planned before creation appear in various rabbinic writings. See examples in M. E. Stone, "The Parabolic Use of Natural Order" in his *Selected Studies in Pseudepigrapha and Apocrypha* (Leiden: E. J. Brill, 1991) 464 n. 17. He sees in this particular list a testimonial to divine control of the eschaton, but he observes that 4 Ezra differs from other Second Temple literature in its lack of personification of the elements of nature (pp. 464–67).

5. Biblical quotations follow the NRSV.

6. Stone includes in v 1, "The beginning is through man and the end is through myself," which the Latin omits, but other versions include in some form. See his textual note in *Ezra,* 142. He understands "beginning" as referring to the end time, which humans will start but God will finish. See his extended discussion of the topic in "Coherence and Inconsistency in the Apocalypses: The Case of 'The End' in 4 Ezra" in his *Studies,* 335, 345–47.

initial bringing into existence of the cosmos but also the specific creation of Zion, the geographical and spiritual center of Judaism; and the
dividing of people into sinners and faithful. The information about the
first two stages is verifiable because they have already taken place; thus
history assures the reliability of his claim that the Deity will bring about
the end time.

Here Ezra highlights two significant aspects of humanity. First, he
foreshadows the theme of election of the Jews by referring to the footstool
of Zion (the center of Judaism) in v 4 as part of the original plan for
the cosmos. Ezra further develops this theme in the third vision, part
of which forms the second passage in this study.

Second, Ezra explicitly divides humanity into sinners and faithful in
v 5. He accounts for sin as estrangement of human imagination, but the
passive verb prevents a clear statement of responsibility for this estrangement. On the other hand, he identifies the faithful as those who store
up treasures of faith, clearly indicating human agency in this case. The
importance of human imagination in making moral choices appears again
in the appendix, in the third passage this study will consider.

The second passage for our consideration is 6:38–59. This passage
appears early in the third vision, in Ezra's address that formally raises
the issues for discussion during that vision. Here Ezra speaks in a two-
part address. He first describes the divine work of creation, then reveals
his assumptions about the priority of his people in the agonized questions, "Why do we not possess our world as an inheritance?" (v 59). Ezra's
speech in this section strongly resembles Genesis 1 in dividing the creation process into six days; each day's work resembles that listed in
Genesis 1. But this passage contains several noteworthy changes and
additions. In the first place, a formulaic expression introduces the work
of each day except the first. The formula indicates the day, then states,
"you commanded," drawing attention to the divine word as the agent
of creation.

Ezra's catalog of the work of each day varies from the Genesis account
at points, and states the purpose of each creature. The first day's work
does not mention the creation of light or its separation from darkness,
(or of the separation of night and day) but assumes it is stored away.
The purpose in the divine command that it be brought out is to illuminate
the divine works. The account foreshadows the privileged position of

humans by commenting on the silence, noting in particular the lack of human voices.

Ezra deviates from the formula "you commanded" in describing the work of the second day. He says, "you created" not the firmament but its spirit, and then commanded that spirit to separate the waters. The purpose is that "one part might move upward and the other part remain beneath" (v 41).

The third day's work includes assigning one-seventh of the space to water and the rest to dry land, to permit vegetation to grow. The appearance of vegetation results from this command; God does not create it directly. The plants are described in sensory detail: he specifically mentions their taste, color, and scent.

The work of the fourth day includes the creation of lights, but in keeping with the first day's work, does not mention the separation of light from darkness. These are assigned the task of serving humankind, again foreshadowing human primacy.

On the fifth and sixth days God commands the water and earth to bring forth living creatures. The discussion of the fifth day's work adds several details to the Genesis accounts. Living creatures come from lifeless water, emphasizing the power of the divine word and offering the nations the occasion to praise God. The mention of "nations" further foreshadows human priority: it implies their eventual creation, their appreciation of other living beings and their recognition that creatures are the work of God. But it also underscores that even the "best" creature serves the creator by praising the divine works.

Ezra adds a discussion of Behemoth and Leviathan, both of whom came from the water like all living creatures. He credits the creator with naming the two monsters and assigning one to live in water and one on land. Ezra comments that the creator will have them eaten at a designated time by particular people, reinforcing the idea of a privileged role for human beings, in this case the righteous, for whom the monsters will become food at the messianic banquet. Humans will finally subdue even the unfettered monsters.[7]

Adam is described in a singular way: there is no mention of his creation

---

7. Stone, *Ezra*, 188. Cf. Job 40:15–41:34; Pss 74:14; 104:26, where the monsters remain unfettered except by divine command.

or of a command as such given to him, nor any mention of complementary sexes. However, Ezra notes that the creator placed the human as ruler over all creation and common ancestor of the chosen people. This last claim is startling: the creation and primacy of humans has been fore-shadowed at several points in the recital of works of creation, but here Ezra leaps from a reference to all people to the more specific designation, "the people you have chosen" (v 54), juxtaposing the themes of creation and election of the Jews.

This recital leads Ezra to the second part of his address and the heart of his point: he claims that God created the cosmos, not for human beings generally but for the chosen people. He emphasizes his point by ascrib-ing to God the declaration that all other descendants of Adam are nothing (vv 55–56). His lament stresses the irony of the Jews' present subservience and ends with the agonized questions, "Why?" and "How long?"[8]

The passage highlights aspects of creation similar to those in 6:1–6. It stresses divine causality, specifically emphasizing the power of the creative word: the creator needs only to speak in order to bring creatures into being. The motif of the creative word receives further emphasis when Ezra asserts that lifeless water responded to the command and produced living creatures (v 48).

The theme of the creator's purposefulness that we noted in 6:1–6 recurs here in several ways. Ezra names the specific purposes of different creatures; notably light will illuminate the divine works and water will bring forth living beings to enable the nations to praise God. Ultimately all creation exists to praise God, with priority of place given to human beings. But then Ezra shifts to a particular group of people, the Jews, as the special focus of creation, bringing together the biblical themes of creation and election. The previous passage alluded to this notion in its reference to the footstool of Zion. Here Ezra focuses explicitly on the notion to emphasize the irony of the Jews' present plight.

In fact, purposefulness is key here on two levels: those of the creator and the author of the book. According to Ezra, the creator made the world for the Jews. And the author's purpose in the book is to wrestle with the implications of the Roman destruction of Jerusalem. By com-bining creation and election themes, the author underscores the irony

---

8. Stone discusses the literary structure of the section in detail (ibid., 181). See also Isa 40:15–17.

of the Jewish situation and in a subtle way makes God responsible for it. If the God who created and chose the Jews is almighty, how can the Romans, who are "nothing, spittle," "a drop from a bucket" (v 56) prevail?

But the author precedes the election theme with an assertion of the priority of the human race: "and over these you placed Adam, as ruler over all the works that you had made; and from him we have all come . . ." (v 54). The passage foreshadows human dignity early in the account, by describing the silence as lack of human voices. Human speech will overcome the silence in the cosmos created by the divine word.

Immediately after attesting human priority Ezra narrows his focus to mention election of the Jews. He concludes v 54, "and from [Adam] we have all come, the people whom you have chosen." By juxtaposing the themes of creation and election Ezra sets the stage for his explicit complaint about the situation of the Jews. He also takes liberties with the notion of universal human priority and splits hairs to distinguish between the dignity of all people and the special place of the Jews, then defends his position by referring to the words of the creator in that regard (vv 55–59). In this vein, it is interesting that the author does not mention the goodness of creation, because the idea could have reinforced the irony of the situation: if what God created for the Jews was good, how could their present suffering be explained?

The third passage, 16:53–63, appears in what is generally understood as an addendum to the book. The section, chapters 15–16, frequently referred to as 6 Ezra, contains miscellaneous oracles of which 16:53–63 is part of the eleventh.[9] This oracle refers to divine omniscience: God knows the sins of everyone; no sinner will escape divine judgment, but repentance can save people from condemnation. As in the previous two passages, the author refers to creation to support the point.

The section begins and ends the creation account with reference to God's knowledge of human beings. The declaration "The Lord certainly knows everything that people do; he knows their imaginations and their thoughts and their hearts" (v 54) introduces the passage. It ends similarly, "He knows your imaginations and what you think in your hearts!" (v 63). Between these two verses a narrowly focused recital of creation

9. For a detailed discussion of the form and origin of the section see Myers, *I and II Esdras*, 112–13; and R. L. Bensly and M. R. James, *The Fourth Book of Ezra* (Cambridge: Cambridge University, 1895) (reprinted in *Texts and Studies* [ed. J. A. Robinson; 3/2; Nendeln: Kraus Reprint, 1967]) lxx–ciii. The eleventh oracle includes vv 52–68.

concentrates on the cosmological: heaven, earth, stars, and particularly water: the sea, springs, pools, and rivers. The only living creatures it mentions are humans, to whom the creator gives a heart, breath, life, understanding and the spirit of almighty God.[10] All creatures came into existence by the words and deeds of the omniscient creator.

The language and imagery describing creation resemble biblical accounts at various points. Measuring the water and assigning it to its place (2 Esd 16:57–58) recalls Job 38:5–8 and Isa 40:12. Stretching out the heavens appears in Ps 104:2, Isa 42:5 and several other passages in Second Isaiah. Springs and pools in dry, high places (v 60) are mentioned in Isa 41:18 and 44:3. Sending rivers to water the earth calls to mind Ps 104:6–8. The formation of humans with breath and life resembles Gen 2:7 and Isa 42:5. And giving humans the spirit of God occurs in Isa 44:3.

The passage contains two significant points relative to creation: divine omniscience and specific gifts to humans. It explicitly discusses divine omniscience, particularly the ability to see into the human heart. And when the Deity reads the heart, it reveals hidden sins (vv 63–65). In addition, the creator "knows the number of the stars" (v 56) and searches and measures (v 57). The section immediately following the creation recital indicates that God will examine human works (v 64), and asks, "How will you hide . . . ?" (v 66). The recital itself implies a knowledgeable creator who fashioned a smoothly running cosmos. This underscoring of the creator's omniscience actually reinforces the attributes of purposefulness and omnipotence emphasized in the previous passages. Purposefulness is as effective as it is informed by knowledge, and knowledge is an aspect of effective power.

In the account human beings alone receive special gifts: a heart, breath, life, understanding, and the spirit of Almighty God. These attributes permit humans to think and imagine, which for the author means to choose between good and evil (v 63).[11] These gifts also imply knowledge, and therefore enhance human dignity by sharing the divine quality of knowledge that the passage underscores. They also temper the tone of the previous two passages, which tend to hold the creator responsible for the present evil situation.

This review of the salient features of the three creation accounts in

10. See also 3:5.
11. See the discussion of 6:1–6 above.

4 Ezra reveals significant information regarding the sets of questions posed at the beginning of this study. Proceeding this time from the particular to the general, the three passages serve a purpose beyond recounting the creation of the cosmos. In each case, in the spirit of a lament, they support the basic question of theodicy that permeates the work, motivating Ezra's complaint about the present condition of the Jews by recalling divine favors in the past. In the first passage he articulates the problematic question of divine versus human responsibility for good and evil. The vagueness of the style expresses his lack of certainty regarding a solution to this dilemma. In the second passage Ezra struggles to articulate a resolution of the conflict with the juxtaposition of the creation and election themes. By attributing to the creator the intention that the world belong to the Jews, a theme that the first passage foreshadowed in mentioning the creation of the footstool of Zion, Ezra leans toward blaming the creator in his agonized question, "Why do we suffer defeat if the world was made for us?" The third passage nuances the dilemma with its conviction that the creator gave humans particular gifts for decision-making. God knows, but does not control, human choices — a thorny reality around which the basic problem of evil revolves. Thus the additions and variations in each of the three passages support the author's concern for theodicy by clarifying aspects of the creator, creatures, and the relationship between them. In this way 4 Ezra demonstrates the significance and adaptability of the creation theme to the current situation.

Because the questions about the theological task and 4 Ezra's faithfulness to the Torah intersect with one another, I will discuss them together. God in the book is one, creator and judge. The divine oneness stands implicit here as in Genesis, but God as creator and judge receive explicit treatment. 4 Ezra emphasizes in a way not found in Genesis that the creator God functions as planner and executor of creation: the planner prepared "these things" (6:6) prior to creating the universe, and then implemented the plan, making and giving a purpose to each creature. This characteristic appears as divine omniscience in the third passage (16:54). The three passages describe creation by word, separation, and craftsmanship. The second passage focuses almost exclusively on the divine creative command that brings into existence and also separates in the manner of Genesis 1, while the first and third describe creative deeds in the manner of Genesis 2. The entire process in all three passages is orderly and purposeful, in the same vein as the Genesis accounts. The creator will likewise carry out events at the end of the world. The orderly progression of the creation process according to the creator's plan and purpose demonstrates the meaning of creator as executor. Finally, God as judge at the end time figures prominently in 4 Ezra, even though that characteristic does not play a major role in creation. The fact that 4 Ezra brings together the two functions when he asserts, ". . . [these things] were made through me and not through another, just as the end shall come through me and not through another" (6:6) illustrates the complexity and subtlety of the author's thought. It also introduces a concern not present in Genesis: the idea of an end time. In Genesis 3 God judges Adam and Eve at the time of their sin; here the author indicates a general judgment at a time in the future that only God knows (4:33–5:13).

The identity of creation in 4 Ezra includes variations from Genesis in the highlighted aspects of creation, in the ways the account is rendered and in its amount of additional detail. Two deletions from the Genesis accounts are particularly interesting: 4 Ezra does not refer to the creation of humans or to the idea that creation is good. Regarding the first of these, the book alludes throughout to the creation of humans (for example, 5:43; 7:21, 70; 8:3, 7–8, 24) but only the third passage, in the appendix, discusses at length the creation of and giving of gifts to humanity. The gifts help people make decisions regarding good and evil, thus increasing human responsibility for evil in the world, including the destruction of Jerusalem in 70 C.E.

Equally telling is the lack of reference to creation as good. Structurally the absence is remarkable because of the other formulaic expressions, particularly in the second passage. But the author mentions neither a divine plan to create what is good, nor an evaluative comment that it was good. Ideologically the lack supports the author's apparent ambivalence over who or what is responsible for the presence of evil in the world.

This ambiguity characterizes the relationship between God and creation, and addresses the third question regarding the theological task. The analysis of the passages suggests that the appendix assigns more responsibility in this regard to humans than does the body of the book, which seems implicitly to blame God for the presence of evil. In effect, the addendum explicitates the dilemma, but tension remains throughout the book over the question. The final section seems theologically to relieve God of responsibility for evil and place more blame (and hence more dignity) on humans.

The book's ambivalence about divine and human responsibility for evil reflects the troublesome circumstances surrounding its composition. The aftermath of the Roman destruction of Jerusalem required a more complex and nuanced account than what is offered by Genesis and 2 Isaiah (which was composed during a comparable time). Second Isaiah insists on divine goodness and power in ways too simplistic for 4 Ezra. Fourth Ezra does not insist on the goodness of creator or creation, but follows Wisdom's way of asking difficult questions about the existence of evil, and points out problematic, complex dimensions of the question as well as suggesting answers.

This discussion demonstrates that 4 Ezra's accounts of creation remain faithful to Torah insofar as one God created in an orderly manner. The basic structure and operation of the cosmos and the creatures that inhabit it resemble the descriptions in Genesis. The purpose of creatures, although more detailed in 4 Ezra, adheres to the normative idea that all other creatures serve humans, who exercise dominion over them. All creation including humans praises God implicitly by its existence, and the human race does so explicitly by mirroring divine characteristics, particularly knowledge and speech, and by praising the creator. But this book presents a more nuanced and problematic creation by telescoping into the Genesis creation theme the notion of election that permeates the Torah, then puts both themes at the service of the theodicy problem that agonized the Jewish community around 100 C.E.

In conclusion, it seems to me that in this case the three interacting sets of questions I posed at the beginning provide a useful framework within which to study the question at hand. They enable the salient features of the passages to surface, and permit discussion of their theological implications within the rubric of creation accounts. They likewise implicitly draw out the universal relevance of the passages insofar as a broad concern over the pervasiveness of evil in the world and responsibility for it continue to engage people of all nationalities and religions. But at the same time, the theme of creation lends itself to this set of questions in ways that other themes might not do. For example, the theological questions about the nature of creation and its relationship to the creator, while universal, pertain explicitly to the creation theme of interest here. They might prove less helpful, or at least less directly relevant, to a discussion of another theme.

Select Bibliography

Albertz, R., *Weltschöpfung und Menschenschöpfung: Untersucht bei Deutero-jesaja, Hiob und in den Psalmen* (Calwer Theologische Monographien 3; Stuttgart: Calwer, 1974).

Allen, J. P., *Genesis in Egypt: The Philosophy of Ancient Egyptian Creation Accounts* (Yale Egyptological Studies 2; New Haven: Yale, 1988).

Anderson, B. W. (ed.), *Creation in the Old Testament* (Issues in Religion and Theology 6; Philadelphia: Fortress, 1984).

———. *Creation Versus Chaos* (Philadelphia: Fortress, 1987).

Angerstorfer, A., *Der Schöpfergott des Alten Testaments: Herkunft und Be-deutungsentwicklung des hebräischen Terminus BR' (bara) "Schaffen."* (Frankfurt: Lang, 1979).

Attridge, H. W., and Oden, R. A., *Philo of Byblos The Phoenician History: Introduction, Critical Text, Translation, Notes* (CBQMS 9; Washington: Catholic Biblical Association, 1981).

Batto, B. F., *Slaying the Dragon: Mythmaking in the Biblical Tradition* (Louisville: Westminster/John Knox, 1992).

Baumgarten, A. I., *The Phoenician History of Philo of Byblos: A Commentary* (Études préliminaires aux religions orientales dans l'Empire romain 89; Leiden: Brill, 1981).

Bottéro, J., and Kramer, S. N., *Lorsque les dieux faisaient l'homme: Mythologie Mésopotamienne* (Bibliothèques des histoires; Paris: Gallimard, 1989).

Brandon, G. F., *Creation Legends of the Ancient Near East* (London: Hodder & Stoughton, 1963).

Clifford, R. J., "The Hebrew Scriptures and the Theology of Creation," *TS* 46 (1985) 507-23.

——, "Cosmogonies in the Ugaritic Texts," *Or* 53 (1984) 183–201.

Collins, J. J., "Cosmos and Salvation: Jewish Wisdom and Apocalyptic in the Hellenistic Age," *HR* 17 (1977–78) 121–42.

La création dans d'Orient Ancien (ed. F. Blanquart; LD 27; Congrès de l'ACFEB, Lille [1985]; Paris: Cerf, 1987).

Crenshaw, J. L., "Prolegomenon," *Studies in Ancient Israelite Wisdom* (ed. J. L. Crenshaw; New York: KTAV, 1976) 1–45.

Cross, F. M., "The Song of the Sea and Canaanite Myth," in *Canaanite Myth and Hebrew Epic* (Cambridge: Harvard, 1973).

Dalley, S., *Myths from Mesopotamia: Creation, the Flood, Gilaamesh and Others* (Oxford: Oxford, 1989).

Ebach, J., *Weltentstehung und Kulturentwicklung bei Philo von Byblos: Ein Beitrag zur Überlieferung der biblischen Urgeschichte im Rahmen des altorientalischen und antiken Schöpfungsglauben* (BWANT 108; Stuttgart: Kohlhammer, 1979).

Eberlein, K., *Gott der Schöpfer—Israels Gott. Eine exegtisch-hermeneutische Studie zur theologischen Funktion alttestamentlicher Schöpfungsaussagen* (Frankfurt: Lang, 1986).

Doll, P., *Menschenschöpfung und Weltschöpfung in der alttestamentlichen Weisheit* (SBS 117; Stuttgart: Katholisches Bibelwerk, 1985).

Gibert, P. *Bible, mythes et récits de commencement* (Paris: Seuil, 1986).

Haag, E. "Gott als Schöpfer und Erlöser in der Prophetie des Deuterojesajas," *TTZ* 85 (1976) 193–213.

Harner, Ph. B., "Creation Faith in Deutro-Isaiah," *VT* 17 (1967) 298–300.

Heidel, A., *The Babylonian Genesis: The Story of Creation* (2d ed.; Chicago: University of Chicago, 1951).

In the Beginning: Creation Myths from Ancient Mesopotamia, Israel and Greece (ed. J. O'Brien and W. Major; AAR Aids for the Study of Religion 11; Chico: Scholars, 1982).

Jacobsen, T., "The Eridu Genesis," *JBL* 100 (1981) 513–29.

Knierim, R., "Cosmos and History in Israel's Theology," *Horizons in Biblical Theology* 3 (1981) 59–123.

Knight, D. A., "Cosmogony and Order in the Hebrew Tradition," *Cosmogony and Ethical Order* (ed. R. Lovin and F. E. Reynolds; Chicago: University of Chicago, 1985) 133–57.

Kramer, S. N., and Maier, J., *Myths of Enki, the Crafty God* (New York: Oxford, 1989).

Lambert, W. G., and Millard, A. R., *Atra-ḫasīs: The Babylonian Story of the Flood* (Oxford: Clarendon, 1969).

——. "The Cosmology of Sumer and Babylon," *Ancient Cosmogonies* (ed. C. Blacker and M. Loewe; London: Allen & Unwinn, 1975) 42–65.

Levenson, J., *Creation and the Persistence of Evil* (San Francisco: Harper, 1986).

Lightman, A., and Brawer, R., *Origins: The Lives and Worlds of Modern Cosmologists* (Cambridge: Harvard, 1990).

Lohfink, N., "The Priestly Document and the Limits of Growth," and "Biblical Witness to the Idea of a Stable World," *Great Themes from the Old Testament* (Edinburgh: T. & T. Clark, 1982) 167–82; 183–201.

Miller, P. D., "Eridu, Dunnu, and Babel: A Study in Comparative Mythology," *HAR* 9 (1985) 227–51.

Perdue, L. G., "Cosmology and the Social Order in the Wisdom Literature," *The Sage in Israel and the Ancient Near East* (ed. J. G. Gammie and L. G. Perdue; Winona Lake: Eisenbrauns, 1990) 457–78.

——. "Job's Assault on Creation," *HAR* 10 (1986) 295–315.

Pettinato, G., *Das altorientalische Menschenbild und die sumerischen und akkadischen Schöpfungsmythen* (Heidelberg: Winter, 1971).

Rendtorff, R. "Die theologische Stellung der Schöpfungsglaubens bei Deutero-jesaja," *ZTK* 51 (1954) 3–13.

Reventlow, H. Graf, "The World Horizons of Old Testament Theology," *Problems of Old Testament Theology in the Twentieth Century* (Philadelphia: Fortress, 1985) 134–86.

Romer, T., "La rédecouverte d'un myth dans l'Ancien Testament: La création comme combat," *ETR* 64 (1989) 561–73.

Sproul, B., *Primal Myths: Creation Myths around the World* (San Francisco: Harper, 1991).

Stuhlmueller, C., *Creative Redemption in Deutero-Isaiah* (AnBib 43; Rome: Pontifical Biblical Institute, 1970).

Van Dijk, J., "Le motif cosmique dans la pensée sumérienne," *AcOr* 28, 1–2 (1964) 1–59.

Von Rad, G., "The Theological Problem of the Old Testament Doctrine of Creation," *The Problem of the Hexateuch and Other Essays* (New York: McGraw-Hill, 1966) 131–43.

——, *Wisdom in Israel* (Nashville: Abingdon, 1972).

Westermann, C., *Creation* (Philadelphia: Fortress, 1974).

——. *Genesis 1-11: A Commentary* (tr. J. J. Scullion; Minneapolis: Augsburg, 1984).

Index

of Ancient Sources

Index
of Authors Cited

Contributors

Bernard F. Batto
DePauw University
Greencastle, Indiana

Richard J. Clifford, S.J.
Weston School of Theology
Cambridge, Massachusetts

John J. Collins
Divinity School
University of Chicago
Chicago, Illinois

Joan E. Cook, S.C.
St. Bonaventure University
St. Bonaventure, New York

James L. Crenshaw
Duke University
Durham, North Carolina

Robert A. Di Vito
Loyola University
Chicago, Illinois

Michael F. Kolarcik, S.J.
Regis College
Toronto, Ontario

Thomas L. Tobin, S.J.
Loyola University
Chicago, Illinois

Gale A. Yee
University of St. Thomas
St. Paul, Minnesota

The Catholic Biblical Quarterly
Monograph Series (CBQMS)

1. Patrick W. Skehan, *Studies in Israelite Poetry and Wisdom* (CBQMS 1) $9.00 ($7.20 for CBA members) ISBN 0-915170-00-0 (LC 77-153511)
2. Aloysius M. Ambrozic, *The Hidden Kingdom: A Redactional-Critical Study of the References to the Kingdom of God in Mark's Gospel* (CBQMS 2) $9.00 ($7.20 for CBA members) ISBN 0-915170-01-9 (LC 72-89100)
3. Joseph Jensen, O.S.B., *The Use of tôrâ by Isaiah: His Debate with the Wisdom Tradition* (CBQMS 3) $3.00 ($2.40 for CBA members) ISBN 0-915170-02-7 (LC 73-83134)
4. George W. Coats, *From Canaan to Egypt: Structural and Theological Context for the Joseph Story* (CBQMS 4) $4.00 ($3.20 for CBA members) ISBN 0-915170-03-5 (LC 75-11382)
5. O. Lamar Cope, *Matthew: A Scribe Trained for the Kingdom of Heaven* (CBQMS 5) $4.50 ($3.60 for CBA members) ISBN 0-915170-04-3 (LC 75-36778)
6. Madeleine Boucher, *The Mysterious Parable: A Literary Study* (CBQMS 6) $2.50 ($2.00 for CBA members) ISBN 0-915170-05-1 (LC 76-51260)
7. Jay Braverman, *Jerome's Commentary on Daniel: A Study of Comparative Jewish and Christian Interpretations of the Hebrew Bible* (CBQMS 7) $4.00 ($3.20 for CBA members) ISBN 0-915170-06-X (LC 78-55726)
8. Maurya P. Horgan, *Pesharim: Qumran Interpretations of Biblical Books* (CBQMS 8) $6.00 ($4.80 for CBA members) ISBN 0-915170-07-8 (LC 78-12910)
9. Harold W. Attridge and Robert A. Oden, Jr., *Philo of Byblos,* The Phoenician History (CBQMS 9) $3.50 ($2.80 for CBA members) ISBN 0-915170-08-6 (LC 80-25781)
10. Paul J. Kobelski, *Melchizedek and Melchireša'* (CBQMS 10) $4.50 ($3.60 for CBA members) ISBN 0-915170-09-4 (LC 80-28379)
11. Homer Heater, *A Septuagint Translation Technique in the Book of Job* (CBQMS 11) $4.00 ($3.20 for CBA members) ISBN 0-915170-10-8 (LC 81-10085)
12. Robert Doran, *Temple Propaganda: The Purpose and Character of 2 Maccabees* (CBQMS 12) $4.50 ($3.60 for CBA members) ISBN 0-915170-11-6 (LC 81-10084)
13. James Thompson, *The Beginnings of Christian Philosophy: The Epistle to the Hebrews* (CBQMS 13) $5.50 ($4.50 for CBA members) ISBN 0-915170-12-4 (LC 81-12295)
14. Thomas H. Tobin, S.J., *The Creation of Man: Philo and the History of Interpretation* (CBQMS 14) $6.00 ($4.80 for CBA members) ISBN 0-915170-13-2 (LC 82-19891)
15. Carolyn Osiek, *Rich and Poor in the* Shepherd of Hermes (CBQMS 15) $6.00 ($4.80 for CBA members) ISBN 0-915170-14-0 (LC 83-7385)

16. James C. VanderKam, *Enoch and the Growth of an Apocalyptic Tradition* (CBQMS 16) $6.50 ($5.20 for CBA members) ISBN 0-915170-15-9 (LC 83-10134)
17. Antony F. Campbell, S.J., *Of Prophets and Kings: A Late Ninth-Century Document (1 Samuel 1–2 Kings 10)* (CBQMS 17) $7.50 ($6.00 for CBA members) ISBN 0-915170-16-7 (LC 85-12791)
18. John C. Endres, S.J., *Biblical Interpretation in the Book of Jubilees* (CBQMS 18) $8.50 ($6.80 for CBA members) ISBN 0-915170-17-5 (LC 86-6845)
19. Sharon Pace Jeansonne, *The Old Greek Translation of Daniel 7–12* (CBQMS 19) $5.00 ($4.00 for CBA members) ISBN 0-915170-18-3 (LC 87-15865)
20. Lloyd M. Barré, *The Rhetoric of Political Persuasion: The Narrative Artistry and Political Intentions of 2 Kings 9–11* (CBQMS 20) $5.00 ($4.00 for CBA members) ISBN 0-915170-19-1 (LC 87-15878)
21. John J. Clabeaux, *A Lost Edition of the Letters of Paul: A Reassessment of the Text of the Pauline Corpus Attested by Marcion* (CBQMS 21) $8.50 ($6.80 for CBA members) ISBN 0-915170-20-5 (LC 88-28511)
22. Craig Koester, *The Dwelling of God: The Tabernacle in the Old Testament, Intertestamental Jewish Literature, and the New Testament* (CBQMS 22) $9.00 ($7.20 for CBA members) ISBN 0-915170-21-3 (LC 89-9853)
23. William Michael Soll, *Psalm 119: Matrix, Form, and Setting* (CBQMS 23) $9.00 ($7.20 for CBA members) ISBN 0-915170-22-1 (LC 90-27610)

Order from:

The Catholic Biblical Association of America
The Catholic University of America
Washington, D.C. 20064